Sat Nam
Jean & David.

Love & Blessings

Guru Singh
+
Guru perkarma
Kaur

DEDICATION

This book is dedicated to all Angels everywhere . . .
To all our Mothers and Fathers – the first Angels in our lives . . .
To Wives, Husbands, Children, Relatives and Friends . . .

This is dedicated to all the Teachers in my world . . .
To Paramahansa Yogananda (my first Teacher) . . .
To Yogi Bhajan (my lifelong Teacher) . . .
To his Holiness the Dalai Lama (a Friend in life) . . .
To Sri AmmaBhagavan (a Friend of life) . . .

We all have Angels -- legions of them -- a very large number.
Some of them walk on all four of their legs . . .
some of them swim in our tanks,
or flutter about our homes and their cages.
All of these Angelic pets and companions accompany us on our
journey of life. GOD bless them while on this Earth
and as our power animals when they move beyond this Earth.

This volume is dedicated to these Angelic tales herein
and to you the readers . . . read in joy

In the new evolution there will be a new economy. Unlike the cutthroat, competitive debt economy of the present world, good-will will be the new currency. Organizations such as The **Guru Singh Global Community** will be the banks that enable the exchange of this currency worldwide. Good-will will be spread around the globe through such banks by creating the gatherings of like-hearted to envision the missions of like minds.

The **Guru Singh Global Community** provides a platform of synchronicity . . . for pioneers, authors, architects, teachers, students, leaders and liaisons of this new evolution . . . sweeping the unifying experience of compassionate conscious prosperity into an active worldwide reality.

THE GURU SINGH
GLOBAL COMMUNITY

Join Guru Singh at http://blog.gurusingh.com/ for the daily Inspirational Blessing and at http://podcast.gurusingh.com/ for Podcasts of current lectures.

Find a collection of his mantra CDs at http://music.gurusingh.com/ and participate in building a strong global community at http://global.gurusingh.com/ . . .

Additional products by Guru Singh:

- **108 Ways to Great Days** – A journey through journaling – BOOK
  As the ancient world grew through its evolutionary progression; yogis, mystics and religious scholars discovered many celestial measurements that involved the number 108. 108 evolved into a sacred recurring theme in diverse spiritual and religious practices around the world as the number of steps from ordinary human consciousness to enlightenment. This book was designed by Guru Singh to have 108 distinct steps. Work with it and enjoy — first the process — then the enlightening results.

- **The Guru Singh Experience Vol 1** // CD Available at www.cdbaby.com
  TRACKS: Ong So Hung, Har Haree, Ek Ong Kar
- **The Guru Singh Experience Vol 2** // CD Available at www.cdbaby.com
  TRACKS:: Ong Namo Guru Dev Namo, Humee Hum Brahm Hum, Aad Guray Nameh
- **Naad Mantra Vol 1** // CD Available at www.cdbaby.com
  TRACKS: Aap Sahai Hooaa, Guru Ram Das, Har Har Har Har Gobinday, Aad Such Jugaad Such, Pran Sutra
- **The Guru Singh Collection** (Guru Singh, Seal & Friends)
  // CD Available at www.cdbaby.com
  TRACKS: I Am, Humee Hum, Fortunate, Wahe guru Golden Temple Song
- **Game of Chants** (Guru Singh, Seal & Friends)
  // CD Available at www.spiritvoyage.com
- **Chantz 2 iMPAct Earth** (mantras to bring light to a troubled time)
  // CD Available at www.spiritvoyage.com

Angels Gather Here

Guru Singh

re™
re•evolution
b o o k s

 Nine Angelic Aspects of Human Life
on Planet Earth

Published and distributed in the United States by: ReEvolution Books
www.gurusingh.com

Printed in the United States of America

ISBN: 1-4515-6334-5

Acknowledgments

DEFINITION - Anxious, fussy, frenzy food: reaching into the future unknown to pull up a reason to worry . . . carefully eaten as a bite size snack. Why not pull up the lightness of wonder -- not the darkness of worry? Wonder invites Angels and solutions into your home.

The Angels help each of us with levity as we deal (on a daily basis) with gravity. Such is the guidance of Angels . . . such are the places in which they gather. Learn to appreciate their gatherings and happily gather there with them.

I want to acknowledge all the help our writings receive from the love and brilliance of many people. Here goes naming but only a few: Guruperkarma Kaur, Sopurkh Singh, Hari Purkh Kaur, Vickie & Brian Boyd, Gurudeep Kaur, Kevin & Nadia Hutchings, Sat Pavan Singh, Randy Haykin, Azita Nahai, Pan, Bean & Juan Carlos, Sada Anand Kaur, Louisa Wu, Michael Sandoval, Paddy Canales, Tony & Sage Robbins, Sam & Lyn Georges and all the other Angels who come and go from the moon to the sun . . . brightening the purpose of existing on this 3rd stone in the system.

I also take this moment to acknowledge those who have been there during the formation of consciousness . . . each of them an Angel in their own way: my friends and foes of childhood; the Turtles of Avalon; my fellow musicians and activists in the 60's Haight; the thousands within 3HO; the millions of Khalsa worldwide; the Blessing givers who have been known, unknown and touched.

To the leaders of the world who have had the task of teaching us how not to be and the leaders of the world who have had the task of teaching us how to be. I am indebted to both of these examples and the Angelic natures in both.

And lastly we acknowledge the heroes and heroines who have passed before us.

Production & Publishing Angels

Editors:
Kevin Hutchings
Guruperkarma Kaur

Art Director - Creative & Production Design:
Sat Pavan Singh

Publisher:
ReEvolution Books

Author:
Guru Singh
Contact and Information:
GSGlobalCommunity@gmail.com

Table of Contents

Prologue

Dreams are always personal, but they are not always logical. We humans are quite humorous when we obscure the light contained by the odd angles of these dreams. Look for the angels that gather in these odd angles; they are there every time and will show you the light if you can laugh.

Do not allow anyone to occupy your dream with the nightmares of their expertise and doubt. But remember: beneath every expert perspective, every personality's opinion . . . there [is] just a person. Learn to relate to the person, no matter what the doubt is in their perspective. Even expert advice can be filled with these doubts and such advice will definitely drive away your dream. But learn to not drive away the doubters; it will be fun to see their faces once you succeed.

When your dream is obscured, know that you are close to it. Look for the humor, gather the angels that are always there, become determined in a blunt, direct way, and bring your dream home. This is your right and it comes along with your dream.

Hunger always arrives to cause the meal to be prepared . . . real food takes time to prepare. There is no such thing as fast food . . . a thing that is to eat is either fast or it is food.

Learn to wait consciously for the answers and responses to your hungers . . . learn to accomplish this waiting with grace. Be aware that: patience is not the art of waiting, it is the science of knowing.

And also remember . . . the bigger the risk -- the deeper must be the prayer and trust . . . and . . . the stronger the prayer, the more Angels show up.

When angels gather they do not converse in false platitudes; they are blunt and direct. Their job is not to chat, but to challenge. Allow the angels that gather in your world to challenge you, otherwise your enemies will, and the experience will contain no light -- not an ounce of humor at all. When angels challenge you, the experience is filled with humor . . . learn to laugh at yourself.

The transition is right now . . . the time is right on . . . the race is here. Use your whole human system to join in this race . . . Angels are waiting to assist you in every way . . . honoring them is essential.

I

Introduction of Angels

Being alive does not change with death . . . it only changes the clothing that life is wearing. Existence is a river and the river exists before it is born. It exists as the rain and the snow in the clouds, as the water in the springs and the lakes in the mountains. These also exist before they are what they are, for existence has no beginning and no end. It is a circle never broken - the river never ends.

When the river of life finally enters the ocean of Infinity, there is a longing left with those who rode on the waters of the river and played in the river's twists and turns and lived with the fun of the rapids and the ripples. There is sadness and joy in the longing of the heart for what was, and there is a knowing . . . that it still is . . . the water of the river does not end when the river is at the ocean.

The Grace of Angels -- reaching into our worlds -- exists in many forms. Do they actually exist however, or do they only appear to? Who are they in the "real" sense . . . some physical . . . some meta-physical . . . some purely imaginary . . . ?

Allow yourself to know that they are all really working . . . they are all really worthy . . . they are all really real! They come to our lives when we are most in need, when we are most innocent and we do not always catch their names, or respond with the ability to pay a full respect. It is said we can thank them and pay them back by passing on the favor to another. That being the case; let's fill the world with Angels, for Angels gather here.

Magic (or miracles) happen when we stop using fear and doubt to interfere with the infinite capacity of the Cosmos. Magic/miracle is in fact the way of the feminine (the Ma the Mir). Logic is the way of the masculine (the Law).

Today's world does not recognize the power of MA (which appears to the untrained senses as chaos). The world is consumed by its obsession with LAW . . . and the predictability of ORDER. This is the world of a child needing the predictability of order to feel safe. This is the world that produces GOD as this disciplinary father figure . . . the world of the exclusive logic.

This attitude will soon be forced from the avoidant grip of humanity as the era changes. This is what we are beginning to experience at this time. The more you are open to magic, the more you will feel centered and at peace in these changing times. The new evolution is one that engages GOD as the balance of both male and female. It is this awareness that opens to the infinite possibility of reality rather than the limited predictability of any particular opinion or cultural fantasy.

Yes: in this more cosmic sensitivity there is an authority that allows us to track all that has been and sort through it to provide the greatest guidance for all that can be. This is the way that those who have gone before us (of all breeds and species) are able to guide us from their loftier perspective. They are known beyond timespace as Angels, guides, fairies and power-animals and they are all around us by the thousands . . . a number known in scripture as Legions. They await our self authorization to secure the connection.

In life we are consistently surrounded by a variety of characters . . . each one bringing lessons. It is never about the character with the lessons . . . it is always about the lessons in the character. The Human psyche has the unique ability to experience THE DOER . . . the reality of GOD. It is good to be a fool, but not an idiot in this endeavor . . . the fool remains neutral and clear and does not make harsh judgment -- the idiot may or may not judge, but does not make sense.

The subconscious is where the engine to your 'desperations' and "demons" lives -- this drives much of your emotional, "knee-jerk" reactions to what takes place in your life story. The superconscious is where the engine to your 'aspirations' and "Angels" lives -- this drives much of your more compassionate and a comprehensive response to what takes place in your life story.

If you are aware enough to know better -- you will be held responsible to know better. When things in your life malfunction . . . it is a message that you are lagging behind on your gratitude. Know better! Spend more time honoring the Elementals -- the Forces -- the Angels -- and the True Self.

If we avoid the pain of knowing better along the road of our mission, we can still fulfill the mission, but we will always repeat the pain. Pain is a resistance to the lessons of time . . . ease is a solution to disease. Simplistic are these angelic attitudes, but oh how real . . . allow them to sink in to your core and meet with the Angels in the process. Embrace your Angels in the midst of those things that hold you back, or else those things will hold you back until you do.

Concern is like a match -- it can light a process. Next step -- blow out the concern before it burns your fingers, and then enthusiasm gathers the fuel for the process you have lit. Angels assist you in the unabashed demonstration of this enthusiasm . . . they are a most helpful relationship in this way. And

remember: the purpose of any relationship is not the relationship . . .
the purpose of relationship is purpose.

If you find the spelling and grammar in this volume to be occasionally strange . . .
enjoy such departures from the standard standards . . . Angels do not follow
the human grammatical rules of APA or MLA much of the time. They do
not speak the way we humans do. We are far too strict in our adherence to
logical formulas. Angels tend to be more free and in that freedom, more
efficient. They attempt to capture the essence of the composition and
deliver the message rather than a rigid obedience to third-party regulations.

Use the left over spaces at the end of each chapter for your own journaling
and memo writing to your Angels . . . they may write you back very soon.

ASPECT ONE

Timespace

ASPECT ONE
—TIMESPACE—

1

What is time? When does a moment of time feel like an eternity? When does forever seem like a moment? What is it that you are experiencing in a great moment? Moreover, in that moment of radiance, of joy, of total enthusiasm — where, what and who are you?

In this huge long or short event of life, time is but the measure of any moment. You have never had the experience of anything other than one moment at a time. All your life you have been experiencing one moment after one moment after one moment . . . and in each of these moments; the time involved is infinitesimally tiny . . . completely lacking dimension.

One thing to be clear about - time is the only thing that you actually own . . . everything else is just a rental, including our bodies. We will all have to return everything when we leave here. Time . . . now this is different . . . you own every moment that you pass through and it is up to you to make the best use of each one of them; because before you know it — there will be no more moments — it will seem as if they never existed.

Time is a construct of our five senses - perceptions within the material multi-verse (the many universes). Time is — at times — an individual opinion . . . at other times it is group-think; it is actually an agreement. You can break this agreement and change the meaning of time. You can change it for yourself and for those around you. In other words, you can take a moment of time and make it so memorable that it is immeasurable.

Since you have the ability to reconstruct time — to change the agreement — you therefore have the capacity to bring pain to zero in any moment . . . and take joy to 100 in any moment. This is the mastery of time. What is your response to this responsibility? How are you going to spend these moments that you own? This is up to you and no one else!

When you are able to use your moments for your momentum and the momentum of those around you, then you are a master of time. You will find yourself in the sweet embrace of fearless wisdom. You will find yourself.

NOTES TO MY ANGELS:

2

Time is an illusion; it might pass like a silent cloud . . . a speeding train . . . like a raging siren, or a gentle stream . . . yet it is always passing - never standing. The passage is not in question, just the sensation it leaves on life with its passing.

How does it leave you? What does it leave you with? When will it return to you? Why was it the way it was?

Einstein and the advanced physicists, as well as the mystics over the centuries, understood that time does not actually exist, that it is simply space moving through a point of reference. In the case of our sensations of time, the human consciousness is that reference point. Great prophets, such as Mohamed, Buddha, Jesus and Krishna, understood that the human heart was the keeper of time . . . they taught that matters of the heart gathered the most value from time, preserved the strongest memories of time and were the best use of our time.

Within the human bio-system the heartbeat is the Taal (the rhythm) keeping a sequence-beat as time moves along its journey. The breath is the voice of the Soul and has a divine song of life to sing . . . if you are able and willing to listen. When this Soul-voice teams up with the rhythm section of the heart, music is created with your life and there is no room for sadness or other depleting emotions.

Sadness is the absence of music - the absence of rhythms - often replaced by the presence of perceptions and opinions which are the accounting of the brain alone. The human brain is like salt in a meal; it will bring out the flavors in the heart-songs - the sensations of time - but if eaten by itself, or consumed in quantities too large for the meal, the brain-salt becomes intrusive and abusive to the taste . . . the song of time becomes a collection of noise.

Matters of the heart are also the most frightening to those who are afraid of the passage of time. Those who are more concerned about the image than the content will move into the emotions that have no rhythm. These are sadness, despair and overwhelm, vengeance, victimization, blame and the likes. These are all sensations of the brain . . . amplifying the senses without extracting the lesson within the experience. Often mistaken as matters of the heart, this sadness and all the other emotions continue forward without rhythm. They are focused on the sensation derived from time without discovering the revelations and prophecies within the sensations.

Though time is an illusion, it is a vitally important illusion to master in this life in the body. For some - measured by time - the life is long and the mastery never arrives. For others, life is very short . . . and the mastery was always there. These are the lives of great masters in our midst . . . often children. These are the lives that bring us the greatest joy to be around and the most powerful lessons to gather from.

These are the samples of lives from the future; future-lives being displayed within this present moment. We see this phenomenon in many of the children . . . these are the lifestyles of the next evolution . . . the prophetic prophets of time beyond our time. Dipping their wings into time-space for however long we are blessed to experience them; we remember them with the greatest of joy. Allow yourself to have time within your heart . . . allow yourself to be with this masterful illusion in the ways of a master.

NOTES TO MY ANGELS:

3

There are some forty to ninety trillion cells in each human body (depending on your size), two-hundred billion in the brain alone. There are cells and molecules — RNA and DNA — the amino acid chains, proteins chains, and chains of enzymes — the crystals of phosphates and glycosylases (salts and sugars), with their labyrinths of light traveling through at a sub-sub-atomic level. The electrochemical, the electromagnetic, the biochemical and bio-mechanical systems all super coordinated and highly synchronized. The human body and life itself, is an elegant immaculate construction of genius.

Can this intricate reality of life be more elegant, more immaculate and more genius than the super-intelligent matrix that gave birth to it? The system that places life into the body and then retrieves it from the body (the cosmic construct known as GOD) certainly cannot be less complex than life itself. This being the logic: why then would we believe that the simplistic stories told over centuries have anything to do with reality. This is the core disconnect between science and religion.

Some of these stories say that you live and then you die . . . it is a sort of lights on — lights off policy. Some billions more, subscribe to the belief that when you leave the Earth — you look a little like fuzzy images of your physical self — then you sit with a harp or flute amongst cool breezes, or a pitchfork in a blast furnace . . . forever. Atheism thrives off these simple undeveloped tales . . . these constructs make no sense when compared to the layers and layers upon layers of intricate systems, bio-instrumentation and forces that keep us alive.

The story of creation with its six days of work and one of rest started out as a parable coded in word-crafting. The interpretations lost their way however, as they were told over the centuries. The only question left worth asking is: what days were being used to measure these events. Not all days are equal you know. A Mercurial day is longer than a year on Mercury. The moon's day lasts forever. Perhaps the story of how this material creation began in seven days was referring to a different measure of a day than an Earth day. A universal day in the ancient stories of the Vedas was originally called a Day of Brahma (Sanskrit for GOD). It was calculated as the time it takes for the core of our universe to rotate one full time on its axis. Just like the twenty-four hour Earth day is the rotation of the Earth on its axis . . . the universal day is the rotation of our universe around its core. This actually calculates in science terms to just under three billion years. The ancients discovered this without any instruments other than the human brain, the human body and some very deep meditations. If you are open to this concept . . . it makes the evolutionary dateline and the creationist dateline somewhat equal — (6 days times just under 3 billion years) — somewhere between 15 and 18 billion years . . . [just like science].

Guru Nanak said there are worlds upon worlds — universes upon universes. Yogis speak of the seven blue Ethers that feed this material multiverse. There is a far more developed concept of GOD awaiting your enlightened consciousness and this one actually calculates and calibrates with science. It is one in which, if you breathe you believe and the measurable components can be explained in rare details, rather than constructed with the misinterpreted contradictions of raw parables.

Remember: These parables were the stories told in code; the traditions connected to these parables preserved their evidence. The parables were never to be interpreted verbatim — this again was far too simplistic — they were sacred clues for wisdom to unfold. The traditions and rituals protected this evidence . . . evidence discovered by awakened masters and prophets in their deep states of meditative ecstasy. These religious traditions and stories can be fully compatible with the science that argues against them . . . if we draw upon the following truism.

'Where there is an impasse and a conflict in any picture; the frame is not large enough — not inclusive enough to accommodate the competing perspectives. Enlarging the frame with facts and research and open dialogs — with debates and experimentation and friendly conflicts — allows for the impasse to ultimately pass . . . for each single picture to fit into the collective frame.'

We are going to build this truism in the days, months and years to come. This is the way of nature and nature has a way of resolution . . . it is called evolution. This is the next evolution. This is a way to move forward toward a time where science and religion, where religion and religion, where nation and nation are all saying the same things in different ways, speaking the same words with different languages, and completing each other's sentences. Where religious and national differences have been the causes of most wars . . . this is where that ends. Nature's inevitable destiny is arriving at peace, resolution and harmony. Will you be a leader, a teacher, or a follower . . . a transistor, a resister, or a transformer in the process? All of these roles are welcome!

4

At the absolute center of everything, there is a point of no dimension that is common to us all. To get here, one must travel on a road of no direction without limitations on the time it might require; you must leave all fears and doubts at the journey's starting point.

This may sound like a riddle, but it is actually a power uniquely human — it uses what is truly the human being's only advantage — our conscious consciousness to be compassionate and One.

As an animal, the human being is not well equipped. We are not fast runners, we are not agile in water, we can't jump very high - not like a cat (five times its body length), or see like a hawk (details at over a mile). We cannot fly on our own, a day old horse can walk, but it takes us over a year to do it. A blood hound has a sense of smell that is 7,000 times more sensitive than ours. We are, in fact, perhaps the least prepared creature for life on Earth.

Why have we been built with such a disadvantage and yet destined to dwell in a world amongst the far better prepared?

The answer lies at our center-point . . . we are not here to master the world outside, we are here to master the world within and then share the world outside with everything. Here in this inner world, there is a sense that is uniquely ours, that is purely human . . . it is a power we are here to lead with. By mastering this inner world we are able to be a leader (not the boss) in the outer world.

The human being has this "extra" sense; a sense of recognizing the importance of the 'commons' (resources vital to all life). And once we locate even a glimpse of these points of our human purpose — like that bloodhound on the scent — our thirst for more is unquenchable, our drive unstoppable.

A few of these 'commons' are Earth, Air, Water, Love, Faith, and Trust and their paths intersect at the absolute center-point of everything. This center-point is the common location for all our relationships of every kind. Here, these 'commons' gather the tribes around the watering holes of love and trust to share the air of the good earth where faith supports life.

Once we release these 'constant commons' from being trade-able commodities, or exclusively possessed fantasies, and realize they simply exist - constant and common for everyone — everywhere - we are then able to follow their "scent" to the center. Here we discover the peace of sharing as if you are as important as I am. We discover calm; we are secure here where we are at one with everyone and everything. In our world . . . all the things we always were, but never allowed ourselves to be, begin to make sense as they arrive.

Practice a daily practice that strengthens your ability to sense the 'constant commons' and share them all around you. Create agreements with yourself and with your friends that allow you to practice sharing Earth, Air, Water, Love, Faith and Trust with great abandon. Discover new members of your tribe on a daily basis and establish an atmosphere that longs to belong together. Be a human being — being human; this is the greatest power of your life on Earth.

NOTES TO MY ANGELS:

5

The illusion of time is in fact an illusion; this doesn't mean however, that it is unnecessary to work with . . . it means it's an illusion, a puzzle, a riddle to master, to work through and to not be ruled by. Remember: when you are unable to make a commitment, the illusion of time is ruling you.

Your position or location on the sliding scale of resolving and mastering this puzzle is known as your karmic account. It will determine the nature of the lessons you must pass through, the experiences you will have, and the obstacles you must overcome to move forward with your life. This shapes the events that happen, the people you meet, the friends and relations you have and the circumstances that prevail and repeat. Knwing this, it is easy to see the reality in the saying: "If it happens to you, it happen through you."

From lifetime to lifetime this karmic account goes with you. When it's transferring from one lifetime to another it's called the samskaras or sanskaras . . . your personal scorecard arrives in this world with its accompanying consciousness. This account actually determines your level of conscious advancement through evolution. One could say that your consciousness is an indicator of your karmas. This is why you should refuse to judge a person because they make decisions you do not agree with . . . judge the message, not the messenger. They have a completely different set of karmas which has led them to a completely different perspective. Their view is right for their karmic position . . . based in their sense of time.

If you were to do nothing about your karmic scorecard, it represents your fate . . . sticking with and stuck in, what you were born with. When you commit to taking on this fate—doing something about it — this fate transforms into destiny. Here, you influence what is given to you as fate, converting and shaping it toward a destination of your choice. This is destiny.

Time and space are the same event. Time is simply the perception of space moving through a single location or point. Time is the movement of space within this limited single perspective and therefore time is mutable . . . change the point — change the perspective — change the time. How you shape this, determines how life unfolds for you. Whether or not you have enough time, a good time, too much time, a bad time, a meaningless time, a valuable time, a meaningful time . . . all is a choice.

Everything that produces your experience surrounds this movement of space through your point of perception. The perspective of your senses is determined by your choices. This is what you control with your outlook and attitude. This is what you control with your decisions to be who you are. This is what you control — your response to the illusion of time through the scorecard of your karma — defines you.

Make a choice — a decision this very day — a decision that makes your day, every day. This is your right and this is your freedom, and the path toward your eventual liberation. This is your choice, and no matter how vague or distant the outcome (the result) may seem; the choice is worth choosing.

Every choice takes place through the illusion of time, if you initiate the attitude and KEEP-UP with your actions, the desired outcome must eventually come out. This is a cosmic law of nature; it has no exceptions. Banking on this is the 'New Economy' — it will be funding the 'Next Evolution'. This is a (non-secret) path to prosperity, the greatest possibility of your life.

NOTES TO MY ANGELS:

6

Living in "normal" worldly consciousness, one perceives and then prefers the perceived to be a particular way — either somewhat different, or a great deal different. This produces the tension of preference — time arises from this tension and agitation. The past is created from a memory of preference in the breath that we are currently breathing . . . hope arises to create a preference of change . . . this defines a time called future.

The thread of time is actually a single thread; it weaves as a single moment through the fabric of all space. All time is of this same moment and all the imaginable space is of this single thread. But because it is never more than one, it has no ability to be perceived . . . perception requires separation. This thread of time is never broken, but perception requires it to break. Consciousness knows where every point is on the thread, but identity requires a mystery to measure against. So, from the perspective of our physical life, the five senses separate the past from the present, and the present from the future. This same illusion separates you from me and both of us from everything else.

We are now living the fantasy of Maya; it happens to us all at about 18 months of age. With the task of breaking this pattern and reconnecting with the cosmos, we set about living our lives to the end. This fantasy has no access to fulfillment, so we seek it through objects. This fantasy has no access to happiness, so we seek it through pleasure. This fantasy has no access to contentment, so we consume. Life is then measured by the caliber of our consumption . . . success is now measured by the 'power-quality' of our 'accumulations'.

"Observation establishes the observed" (said Einstein) — "all positions and opinions are controlled by your observation" (said The Buddha). Because your observation is asking for this world to change and become your preference — you do no longer perceive what is; you now perceive the tension created by the absence of your preferences. You have broken the thread of higher consciousness and disconnected from the continuum of your experience. This firmly establishes your identity as a marker . . . your preferences define your place in the world. This is all very painful, but will ultimately become a gauge . . . a measuring device demonstrating precisely how far you have progressed and how far you have yet to go in the evolution of your consciousness.

This illusion must be unraveled and re-woven by the progression of your consciousness. It is not separate . . . it is but one thread . . . and when your perception becomes without preference, you will begin to resolve the observation of separation.

This is the purpose of your life, with all of its illusionary displays, and all its circumstances and its dilemmas. The goal is to reweave this single thread back into the full fabric of life, to regain the innocence seen in the newborn baby's eyes. The innocence that is constantly saying, "We are one . . . we are one." This innocence causes you to care unconditionally for the newborn. This innocence is the greatest power of all.

Innocence — means: "in the sense of zero" (no separation — no preference) . . . in-Ø-sense. Zero — the unbroken thread of time-space — without beginning — without end — woven throughout the cosmic cloth. Our purpose is this innØcence — reconnecting with it all.

Such is the awareness of perception without preference — the goal of our highest consciousness. This might seem beyond your comprehension from a preferential perspective, but nevertheless, it is a perfect goal.

NOTES TO MY ANGELS:

7

How many times have you caught a ball? Do you know that we do not actually 'catch' a ball — we set up and wait for the ball to arrive? It is all the calculations and calibrations before the ball arrives — no matter how short or long this takes — that determines the accuracy and attitude of the catch.

This is the same as in life. We set ourselves up and life arrives through time-space. You must accept your right to have your life in order for you to set your life up for the catch. Life — a period between birth and death — is waiting for the ball of expectations to arrive in the hand each day. Be absolute in your expectations of excellence.

When you stop holding the world around you to its old capacities and expectations, it can develop new ones in your presence. This is the power of time . . . never living in the past, but being present for the future to arrive in the hands of your present moment.

Present time was the first to arise from creation's instance. Then — within a moment of no dimension, in the gap left by time's creation — the past created space. It was all happening very fast — instantaneously by our measures — with no vacuum permissible in space, matter filled the void and it all seemed very real.

Such was the first moment of creation and this is the first to go when you go from here. From nothing we came and back to nothing we go. Time constructs all space and in this space, the cycle of matter rises and falls. Every moment is a birth, a death and a rebirth . . . matter coming and going through time. The ball of life flies through space and arrives on time, every time. There are moments when the absolute is absolutely everything, and there are moments when absolutely nothing is absolutely necessary.

Passing through these moments will sadden and depress you if you are attached to the ball of stagnation . . . non-movement. If you are flexible with movement, you will find joy in these cycles. In the death of the present-present, is found the hope of birthing the future present. Set yourself up in the field of your life and wait for the ball to arrive in your glove of this time. Such are the joys of this new way of viewing the reality of who we are . . . in this the next evolution. After all — materially — from nothing we come and to nothing we go, but we are really 'something' forever . . . we are forever GOD . . . in what ever form you envision that to be. That is the "catch!"

NOTES TO MY ANGELS:

8

In meta-physics, we know that the universe is only a part of a far vaster multi-verse. Each individual universe within this multiple system has its own central sun, the "bang" driving creation forward. Like bacterial spores in a petri dish, these spots of creation have sprouted in more than one location at once. Like the bacteria in the petri dish, the entire system is constantly growing, multiplying and expanding.

Beyond these material points is what we refer to as the infinite void . . . endless zero-space . . . or shunya (Sanskrit).

All of this operation is continuously generating matter to this day, conducting this production of the five elements and the five forces and the countless conditions that maintain this material world . . . all recognizable to our five senses. There are worlds upon worlds within these dimensions, extending on beyond anything that we can possibly measure.

From this outward view of the macro worlds, there is also an inner view that reverses back down through matter into the miniature perspectives of the micro-worlds . . . the cells and the atoms and the sub-atomic particles. This entire system — outward and inward — is self-organizing . . . chaotically, chaordically and orderly. It is chaotic when it needs destruction; it is chaordic when it needs re-generation and it is orderly during the brief points of each life.

Our human free will sits in the middle of this entire operation. It sits there actually thinking that our world and our involvements in the world are of great importance. If you can actually comprehend the vastness of this entire system you will have to conclude that your circumstances are but an immeasurable blip on the screen of it all. What you are is only meaningful to the whole — when you are in tune with the whole. When you are out of tune, out of harmony and at odds with this infinitely vast system — you are meaningless . . . literally without meaning . . . just a speck of dust . . . a smudge on the clarity of creation.

Every day it is up to you to become tuned up, in tune with this giant and make your life meaningful to this enormous construction. Have a role in its unfolding by becoming an asset to the creation of creation. Relax and surrender to its vastness. Relate to it through your daily routine. Become a micro-bit of the gigantic event, and in this way you will connect to joy, enthusiasm and your fulfillment. This is the next evolution of human consciousness . . . this is the greatest possibility of your life.

NOTES TO MY ANGELS:

ASPECT TWO

Conscious
Awareness

ASPECT TWO
— Conscious Awareness —

9

There are five levels to the full development of human consciousness; it is scheduled to unfold within the following chronology: 0 to 3 years old — envy and frustration; 3 to 7 years old — jealousy and anger; 7 to 12 years old — observation and determination; 12 to 18 years old — imagination and inner-quest (self realization); 18 years and older — inspiration and commitment to purpose.

It is obvious that few people pass through all five levels. Most people are (what is called) developmentally arrested (stuck) at some stage along the way; they arrive at where they are comfortable with surviving and stop growing . . . mostly in the first three levels.

Beyond this is an extremely advanced and arduous course and to complete its entirety is the mastery modality. Achieving all stages of development is as if you have graduated from graduate school with several PhD's.

Being in the higher stages of conscious development requires tremendous discipline; whereas the lower levels only require reactions to life. You must not judge anyone from the levels below your standard . . . any more than you would judge a first grader because you are in the twelfth grade. To judge is a reaction, not a higher observation.

As one can see, the majority of this planet is satisfied to simply be in reaction to what takes place. Because of this, Earth is just like a one-room schoolhouse . . . all 'grades' of development contained on a single planet. This means that there are going to be many attitudes and conflicting opinions since not everyone is able to comprehend all the subjects and topics that are occurring in the vast complexities of life on Earth.

For this reason it is incumbent on all those who are of a higher consciousness and understanding to become as teachers in the 'One Room Schoolhouse'.

The rules of the successful teacher in such a one-room affair are those of compassionate communication and patience. This is the standard of leadership required for a planet with such diversity and levels of development. This is not the simple response, it is the successful one; this is not the easy response, it is the effective one, and if you are in a higher stage of development, you must become one of the effective and successful leaders . . . not a judge shouting from the sidelines.

Work to achieve the highest level of your personal development and do so while remaining judge-less, compassionate and effective in your leadership. Remember: being judge-less does not mean being unaware . . . it means that you do not condemn that which your awareness leads you to see. This is the radiance of the new evolution of human consciousness . . . this is the pathway to the greatest possibilities of life.

NOTES TO MY ANGELS:

10

When you walk into any room, make it your home. Then help every one in the room to feel at home. Remember, you are uniquely you and you have every right to be exactly that. Do not try to fit in, you fit perfectly in you.

In the course of human life - under "normal" consciousness - we access the collective ancient human mind's base survival frequencies through the random nature of our inclinations.

In this way we live in our fate. This is you walking into the room . . .

When we are inspired to seek guidance from our higher consciousness; we access much higher frequencies of the collective ancient human mind. As an individual incarnation we achieve this through our sacred disciplines. This is you standing in the room . . . feeling as if you are home.

This opens the miraculous world of our destiny, far beyond the limitations of our fate. This is you making everyone else in the room feel at home . . .

It is the very reason why sacred disciplines are essential. Yoga and meditation - to reconstruct our random inclinations - are mandatory for the next evolution of humanity.

NOTES TO MY ANGELS:

11

Safe is a state of being, not a place. It is a state that invokes feelings that in turn invoke perceptions, which create a sense of the pace at which time appears to pass. These feelings — perceptions - and the pace — all influence the value of the "place" . . . you perceive as your location. This is a state of being and your question is . . . is it safe?

The value of pace, like place, creates an opinion. Is it a good time, a bad time, a real time, a fast time, not enough time, too much time and much more? Place and pace ultimately determine who you think or feel you are — which you interpret as who you are. This is not actually who you are, it is how you appear through this system of filters, but this is only your observation, something far away from you.

Because you appear to be something other than what you are; you have a feeling inside of being out of place, out of sorts and out of time. You don't feel cozy. You try to correct this with all sorts of changes and consumptions, but it is like that unreachable place on your back. Nothing you do can get to it.

When you don't feel cozy, you project this lack onto your surroundings and this in turn reflects a lacking back on you. This cozy-less reflection comes back from everything and everyone in your vicinity and now you feel uncomfortable with them too. You blame it on "them" — but it is not them.

Such is the formation of life. It has nothing to do with anything other than you. If it happens to you, it happens through you. But you cannot determine this when you are influencing everything with your projection formed through these deceptive filters. Further: when you also prefer this to be different; you do not actually see this for what it is — you see this through the distortion of your further desires.

This we call the dance of Maya. It is a bias and is nearly one hundred percent pandemic in this world. Our job, as humans, is to reduce this chaos and bias and ultimately see things as they are, not as they appear. When you can get to viewing things as they are; you will perceive everything without wanting it to be different. This is a difficult puzzle. This Maya . . . this puzzle, is a code that yogis have sought to break forever. Not only does this pertain to everything and everyone around you; it also pertains to you, because everything reflects you back to you.

Spiritual writings refer to desire-less-ness . . . not to be without intention, but to be without distortion. Desire-less-ness is perception without preference . . . a view of the world, including you, without distorting the picture with these illusions of bias. Such are the twists of a human existence and it is up to you to break the code . . . with yoga, meditation, contemplation, chanting, prayer and anything else you can use as your daily disciplines.

NOTES TO MY ANGELS:

12

We arrive at any and all conclusions via a complex subset of micro decisions . . . that lead to larger sub decisions . . . that work their way up to decisions . . . then macro decisions and on to conclusions and eventually hardened opinions. Most of this takes place in the subconscious brain, some in the conscious brain, but all by a chain of unconscious psychological commands. Some of this is even controlled by our ancestors through their DNA in our glands and organs . . . the glands and organs that produce our emotions and our feelings.

Any angle of observation — current or past — during this entire complex process; any immeasurable subconscious micro-conclusion that is slightly off center, can dramatically alter the outcome. This is why, even when we condemn the message, we must never condemn the messenger.

Understand: everyone has come to their conclusions through this intricate pattern and process. Condemnation will not convince anyone of anything. To change an opinion will not be easy and the simplicity of condemnation is definitely not enough to accomplish this, or anything of value for that matter.

Respecting the messenger is a great place to start if changing the message is important. Communicating about the disagreeable message is best begun by asking respectful questions of the messenger . . . questions about how the conclusions were arrived at. Allowing both you and the 'other' to reassess the angles during this process can have a far reaching result . . . even the discovery that the (so called) "invalid" position might have a set of valid points.

This is the flexibility of solution. Water arrives at its goal (the ocean) by passing through many obstacles along the rivers and waterways of its journey . . . it does this through its supreme flexibility. Whatever the obstacles might present, flexibility locates the answers. Solutions always produce a greater awareness. This is why water is called a solution. This is the path of a solution on its way to the ocean of peace and calm amongst adversaries. This is the way life creates unity amongst great diversity. This is the future of our world if the world is to survive. This is the future of all our relationships if they are to survive.

This requires tremendous courage, time and focus ... we must be there now ... and make the 'there' right 'here' ... and make the 'when' right 'now'. Accomplish this by continuously re-achieving your center-point. Your daily practice is the perfect path to consistently re-achieving this center-point. It brings peace and gives you the tools to bring peace to the mutual perspective. This mutual perspective — the collective message of the various messengers — will then work magic on the diversity of these messages. Each message will become its greatest projection all by itself and in this greater projection, solutions are located magically. This is the nature of magic, which is half of our universe.

This is the next evolution of human consciousness . . . this is the greatest possibility of understanding life and of understanding death. This is when GOD is not only the Father, but the Father and the Mother. This is . . . .

NOTES TO MY ANGELS:

13

Our physical world is a lifetime of learning that . . . you have come . . . and you will go. One of the fundamental laws of this world is the impermanence of the physical body; it displays the permanence of spirit and if you are upset by the impermanence of this world, you are constantly struggling against spirit. You are un-tuning your physical instrument and fighting what is.

Each of us has a core melody and a core rhythm. It is our song of this life and we came into this world to play it. You didn't come into this world to copy mine, or play anyone else's. But if your instrument is out of tune - even if you know your song very well - you will not be able to play your song harmoniously. This is the importance of health and consciousness.

When you begin to align with the harmonic convergence of your song, you become intuitive. Intuition is not good guessing . . . intuition knows beyond the rational. You know because you know and that is that. When your instrument is fully tuned, you not only live harmoniously in time space, but you know beyond timespace.

With an un-tuned instrument, there tends to be more aggression and frustration, which leads to a further need for dominance. This creates the malfunctions of societies with their main emphasis of life becoming the struggle for law and order. Just like today's world . . . we have now entered the era where nothing will work out until the instruments of humanity are tuned.

Those reading this are perhaps more in tune than most, but that doesn't make us better, it only makes us more in tune. We may feel less in tune at times, but that is because we are more aware. It is time we further tune our own instruments.

We all have a core value. We all have a core song at the center of our being; it governs our tendencies and our expectations. We need to move through the debris that has surrounded this song for generations . . . for lifetimes . . . the debris that has kept us out of tune and out of touch. When we become more in tune, we will then have additional responsibility. The word is actually response ability . . . moving through timespace with the ability to respond. This is the sign of leadership, the sign of a teacher and of mastery.

This leadership has confidence, is deeply benevolent, and is completely centered and highly intuitive . . . this leadership is able to guide all life forward. The instrument of this leadership plays the songs of life in harmony, because the instruments are well tuned. This is the leadership of inspiration with the coming era . . . the era of the new economics in the next evolution. This is a change we can all bank on, we can invest in. This is the new prosperity . . . advancing the greatest possibilities of life. This is the new evolution of human consciousness.

NOTES TO MY ANGELS:

14

Living life beyond the need to run and search and chase and defend your position is a matter of surrendering to a universal agreement. Such an agreement recognizes your Divine Right and the Divine Right of all life to be. Chasing after, hiding under, or arguing over, all stem from doubting the existence of such an agreement. It is ultimately a self doubt . . . an anger that is being used to force others into verifying and approving your right . . . the very rights that are already yours.

There is a self value missing here . . . a foundation that you do not believe in yourself. Due to this missing component, a series of lessons will automatically be presented in your life in order for you to ultimately live beyond the need for this approval. These lessons will be as painful or painless as your impulse to surrender or resist them. These lessons are a guarantee - the outcome will be determined by your surrendering, or your resistance . . . your preservation, or your commitment.

The pathway to mastering these relentless lessons is the pathway of true and unconditional surrender. This can be the most feared form of all surrendering . . . a painful or painless process depending on the level of your resistance. This commitment projects life beyond the 'identity-fears' of self preservation. When such a commitment is permitted, one recognizes all of ones own connection-desires hiding behind the massive loads of self defense . . . like a fearful child behind a mother's dress . . . refusing to emerge into the surrounding joy.

This is the fear of losing the image and the identity - the fear of change. It blocks relationships from being ships and maintains them as canoes and when in a canoe you can never stand up. Don't be fooled; of course everyone wants change, they just don't want it to be too different.

One of the fastest ways to abandon and leave this defensive, fearful, confused and childish world behind is by being fully present at the birth of a child itself. With this event comes the inherent and very real discovery - "I" am the value "I" am - all life is a Divine Right - surrendering is a victory - and your capacity of commitment is boundless and ultimately all pain is painless. Arriving at this boundless capacity to commit, you are introduced to the limitlessness nature of your strength.

Within this limitlessness discovery of your strength, you tap the omniscient layers of potential, and within these layers of potential is contained the constantly present - utterly sensible joy. A reality that dwells inside each cell of all life (plant and animal) and when consciously experienced, it stops your pursuit of the endless "chase" and allows you to come back home to relax.

This "chase" always wants you to: find the way - defend the position - prove the argument - claim the right - discover the secret - find the happiness - locate the right person - become and experience the ultimate desire of the most elegant phenomenon . . . so many requirements. This is the pathway of endless exhaustion, constant frustration and absolute illusion. Leave this chase - sit in one place - claim your right by surrendering your free will to your total commitment . . . not to an object (target of your "chase"), but as the subject of being you and having the right to be just that.

This is your immortal authority coming to life. This is your Divine Right of Life deciding to live. This is truly earning a living and can be discovered in the innocent command of babies. This deserves no defense, no argument, no approval of the infinite nature of its value. This is the universal agreement requiring no chase, but requesting total surrender.

Will you surrender your 'SELF' today?

NOTES TO MY ANGELS:

15

Seek new perspectives through your flexibility — physical, emotional
and psychological flexibility. Greatness does not arrive through great
variety — discovery does not appear through endless travels.
Great discovery arrives through seizing the momentum of a single moment
within a single space . . . this is a new perspective.

But is it the perfect discovery, or even the best one? The answer . . . is not
an answer, but a realization.

Perfection is the flexibility of absorbing the imperfections into the soul of
each moment . . . backing yourself into the imperfectly uncomfortable
corners where your greatest strengths are discovered. When you are
emotionally flexible — instead of emotionally reacting in fear and anger, or
retreating into sadness — you create the perfections that absorb everything
standing in the way of your connection to your greatest strength.

What you believe you are not strong enough to handle is only the illusion
of your own inaction. Make each uncomfortable corner that arises in this
process as your home — not a threat — and learn through this experience
to dwell in the collective home of every single moment as a guest — not
wandering the world searching as a ghost.

Avoid the discomfort and shock of your own impermanence by identifying
with the permanence of these strengths that have been gathering around
life and your life forever. Learn to evolve through the process of evolution,
not the access to great variety and exciting escapes. You actually know by
now that all escapes are futile.

It is the complete lack of any escape plan (being trapped in a corner) that
creates the creative strengths for dealing with any single moment until that
moment is successfully fulfilled. Having access to run through the outside
world at will, is an attempt at postponing your growth until it is comfortable.

Well — it will never become comfortable. The laws of 'cause and effect'
(karma) will insure this.You are here to grow, and the external comforts
have never been evolution's growing fields. True comfort arrives when you
have passed all tests of discomfort and are able to be completely

comfortable anywhere-anytime. You only believe you are not strong enough to achieve this because you have never allowed yourself to sit in this corner long enough for the proof of your phenomenal ability to arrive . . . you actually can do this.

Access the voice of these massive inner strengths by listening to their heartbeat as an absolute guarantee — not running to seek them out — but being with them. Trying not to react is futile and impossible at this moment — having nothing to react to is the nature of the path. This is the goal of your growth and the goal of your growth is the purpose of your life.

The foundation of all this cornering and growing and strengthening is self-compassion. It can never be a target or a goal. It is a by-product of simply being real — in real-time. Self-compassion — the highest form of human behavior — is the state of being seen by the self as perfect through the imperfect views of your eyes and the eyes of others . . . seeing your "self" as being perfectly-imperfectly-perfect in the mirror of the material reflection. With these views come the solace and grace and comfort beyond any imaginable comfort . . . the state that life and your life have been pursuing since the BANG.

Welcome to the New Evolution . . . Welcome to YOU!!!!!

NOTES TO MY ANGELS:

16

When you move on pace with Pace ((capitalized Pace is the pace of nature, the world, and the Cosmos)); there is no struggle, there is no resistance, and there is no pain. When you move at the pace of Pace you are riding the Wave of Time - perfectly balanced through the Sea of Space with grace and ease. There is no differential measurable by the nature of inequality known as tension, pressure, friction, stress, disgrace or disease. Moving at the pace with Pace is to be in tune with all that is present and all that is arriving to be present.

This is what Lord Krishna said to Arjuna in the Gita . . . " [. . . .] accept your place in this time and space and you will fulfill the destiny (the purpose) for which life was gifted. Fight against this purpose and your life is destined to be a struggle [. . .]."

When you move slower than Pace, there is sadness and depression. When you move faster and more frantic than Pace, there is frustration and anger. All of these are also available as tools to make slight corrections, or even major ones. But they are not positions to live in constantly. Make certain that you are not constantly paying these stressful prices; it will ultimately have an adverse affect on your emotional, psychological and physical health.

When you must move faster or slower than Pace - then you must be OK with your anger or your sadness. This is a fair price to pay for an equal outcome. When there is a required/desired outcome; you must pay the price willingly and be good with this price. Do not complain about such a price - you sought the outcome, or you were unconscious in your efforts and mistook/misplaced the outcome - either way - now is the time to pay the price. The universe is an absolutely accurate accountant when it comes to the principles of Karma.

Remember: if it happens to you, it happens through you.

When you are sad or when you are angry, do not attempt to avoid or distract these emotions. It is the messenger of inequity; it is telling you that THE world and YOUR world are not balancing. Either you must shift your effort, or shift your desire, or shift your perception . . . work with these and locate the reasons for this required shifting. Re-discover the most efficient pace.

Whatever is required, pass through it elegantly with integrity - get back in touch and in tune with the Pace of the world and the Cosmos. Return from sadness and anger to your rightful place in happiness . . . happiness is your birthright . . . the greatest possibility of life.

NOTES TO MY ANGELS:

17

There is always a cosmic chatter surrounding each of us; a collective, Etheric conversation that promotes and denotes our vision ... all the reasons and every detail directly corresponding to our intentions. When this appears as resistance to progress, what question do you ask? (1) Why is this blocking me ... or ... (2) Where is this leading me?

Remember: resistance is only resistance when you resist it. When you embrace it, it transforms into guidance. The second question is an embracing one.

Intention is a handle onto which life is able to grasp. Guided by this cosmic chatter, life takes hold of your intention. This might feel contrary to your intended direction, counter to your pre-determination, or even chaotic. Remember, these are the winds of change — a force to be used — and as such, it is up to you to use it — not consumed or disrupted or disgusted or disgruntled by it. The result will lie in your interpretation.

If this was the only piece of advice bringing chaos to conclusion, or intention to realization, would you not want to join it? [. . . .] It is up to you to trust this question [. . . .] It is up to you to allow your character to trust the chaotic process known as transformation . . . even though you are not certain of the new formation.

The Cosmos knows who you are; the Cosmos knows where you are and where you want to be. This is the nature of nature — this is the law of nature — this is a cosmic principle. You are not outside these laws. You are not being forgotten by this nature. You are not an exception to this rule.

Pose a conscious question into this chatter and breathe. Do not breathe like you are taking it, or owning it, but as if you are receiving it as a gift. Receive each gift of breath at the very tip of your nose and sit in the middle of the resulting sensation. Become the experience of your breathing, not the breather, or the producer of the breath. When you are able to master this meditation, you are the essence of your existence. Your psyche will now gain access the 'collective human conscious mind' to become psychic and intuitive.

This 'collective human conscious mind' is like an ocean, there to serve you with all the knowledge you require. Your conscious breathing is the pass-code to this infinite database. Learn to use this intuitive access and then guide the chaotic forces surrounding you. Suddenly, nothing that has always been around you — everything at your disposal — resistance or assistance — all the chaotic events — none of it seems foreign, or random, or even threatening. Because of the shift in your perspective, they now appear to be helpful and endearing . . . fear is not needed to control them, or doubt required to subdue them.

Everything that once felt threatening now appears as an asset. The only thing that has changed is your perspective. All this time you were being given assistance . . . you were interpreting it as resistance. It was never amongst the facts that you were lost; it was amongst your interpretations of these facts.

Welcome [now] to the "new" reality that has always been here. Welcome to the loving nature of nature that has always loved you. Welcome to your life that is here to fulfill your dreams and all you intentions. Welcome to the gifts you are being given. Welcome to you within you . . . the new evolution of human consciousness.

NOTES TO MY ANGELS:

18

Innocent children invest no capital or judgment in being wrong. They are simply wrong when they are wrong and 'OK' with that . . . no guilt, no shame, no capital, no judgment.

Innocence is one of the keys to learning . . . being wrong - some of the time - is a guaranteed event while learning. It indicates courage. Courage is a word that means - coming from the heart and at the heart of the game is the fulfillment point.

Remain a student throughout your life . . . be constantly willing to begin at a beginning as a beginner. Then be happily wrong to become happily right . . . invest your capital in the right of eventually discovering right. It is an adventurous and rewarding path and honors your highest self.

NOTES TO MY ANGELS:

19

We are always in the midst of evolution. Every move and every thought we incur registers in the evolutionary equation and contributes to the collective human mind. Evolution does not honor our weaknesses; therefore, when we practice weakness without striving to correct it, we set our self up for "disposal" (being rendered meaningless). All the time we spend in this state is non-time; it is life wasted. This is not saying to feel bad about mistakes — quite the contrary . . . mistakes are not weakness, they are opportunities created from courage . . . the courage to attempt something new or challenging. Feel great about your mistakes and use the opportunity to courageously make corrections.

Remember: weak orientations do not automatically align. If they did, nature would simply spiral down into non-existence as one weak trait after another enabled demise. Humans are the only creature in creation who believes weakness will be lifted to the goal out of pity. No other creature has this mistake in their brain.

We are — by nature and by the new evolution — 'homo-sapiens' on a journey to becoming 'homo-deva' (pronounced homo day vah) This is human beings becoming gods on Earth. We are not to become the ONE GOD, but holographic replicas bringing Heaven to Earth.

We are not on this journey automatically however . . . until we overcome our lower frequency animal trigger points of betrayal, abandonment and rejection, we are still floundering in the old competitive evolution of animal survival. These triggers have also been in the collective human mind for eons. They work like this: when events outside the self go faulty, we feel betrayed; when parts of our inner world (body, mind or emotions) go faulty, we feel abandoned. In these weak emotional states, we trigger our revenge or our victim. In this state of mind, all our external mechanical difficulties and breakdowns invoke a sense of betrayal, while health problems invoke a sense of abandonment . . . the body abandoning you when you need it . . . like in death. In order to simulate a sense of being in control, we employ rejection — we reject before we can be abandoned or betrayed. In this way, we limit our emotional exposure, but also our evolutionary progress, lifetime after lifetime after lifetime.

This is the very reason that - Guru Nanak - Jesus - Mohamed - The Buddha - and many other Prophets taught that the highest form of living is to live as if you are already dead. You do not go about as a corpse; you go about as spirit having a physical experience. In this way, you face every facet of your world while intuitively understanding each detail . . . before, during and after it takes place — no blame — no claim.

This is the state of God consciousness, Christ consciousness, Guru's Grace — so many words describe it. This is the goal of every religion and every spiritual path. This is the human state of homo-deva . . . invoking the Divine Presence.

To practice this on a daily basis, take the time to sit for a few minutes at the beginning of each day and bring yourself to stillness inside and out. Be motionless and silent and allow the messages for your day to unfold. The more you work at this the better you will become. At first, it will seem like just more noise from the days before, but after doing this for several weeks, on a daily basis, you will begin to experience a sense of levity and authenticity in the messaging.

Join in the joy . . . become a partner of the Heaven on Earth team.

NOTES TO MY ANGELS:

20

Normal tends to muddle along in the unconscious fog directly behind the land of law and order and control. The insanity of genius has a territory that comes with very un-normal consequences. Your task in the midst of your genius is to joyfully manage these consequences.

Compassionately discredit your aversion to such consequences and openly accept their ingenious discoveries. Retrain your responses to serve this more elaborate vision.

Since the reality of humanity is a combination of our animal nature and the cosmic nature . . . bring more of the cosmos into your natural state. Present these elevated options and then represent this same elevation with your thoughts, words and actions.

Do not become upset with the dilemmas this magnifies. Allow the access to such magnification to also magnify the discovery of incredibly un-normal solutions. This will make it possible for multiple billions to live as one on this planet.

NOTES TO MY ANGELS:

21

Where you are actually located right now in this life is what is referred to as your fate ... the actual conditions and consciousness and emotions and thoughts of this very accurate — yet un-progressed and un-regressed —moment.

Your destination in this life . . . the reality of who you ultimately are — who you can become through all your activated options — is referred to as your destiny.

The journey of a human life is to travel from where you are — your fate — to who you are — your destiny.

Most people consciously or unconsciously distract themselves from living in either of these locations. They are neither where they are, or who they are, but a chaotic mixture of being distracted from the actualities of fate and doubting the possibilities of destiny. All this while life - patiently and dutifully - waits on some parallel track . . . waiting for consciousness to awaken to at least one of these opportunities.

The process of destiny has forever ... the awakening however, will take place in a single given moment ... welcome its arrival with all your heart and with every breath.

NOTES TO MY ANGELS:

22

Among the four channel-lenses (Feeling, Perception, Pace and Place) through which our world as humans is experienced; Perception and Pace (head and heart) are the two that have the most to say about the quality of our experience. Feeling defines the flavor . . . Place the demeanor. When the rate is coordinated between the Pace of your life and the Perception of all life itself; your balance becomes that of excellence . . . connection to everyone and everything supports you with caliber.

Use the long counter balance pole of moderation (the middle path as both the Buddha and Guru Nanak taught), it allows you to walk on this high-wire of life's supreme excellence without falling off the stage of your existence. To do this: slow down — create a 'practice' that synchronizes your brain rate and heart rate — allow for accuracy to persist in your vast manifestations . . . countered by a strong commitment to resist the equally vast temptations. "For every action there is a reaction of equal value" . . . temptations are therefore attracted to every life among the stratospheric high-wires. They are the bees drawn to the sweetest flowers of your ecstasy.

The stratospheric high-wire is the maximization of your dreams . . . it is not for everyone . . . when many venture there, the result is many fall. Look at all the heroes throughout history in our world . . . so many tragically leaving before it seems they should go. This is why the high-wire is attempted by so few . . . life lived by most is from the middle of the pack.

If you want to go out into that stratosphere . . . if you want to walk the high-wires of your life and breathe that rare air; you will have to arrange your personal affairs with great equilibrium, poise, stability and steadiness to accommodate the constant confrontation that will join you at those heights.

Provide an enormous song and phenomenal dance before you fly into the Sun.

NOTES TO MY ANGELS:

23

Remember when the world was flat? Ignorance created that flat world out of one that was perfectly round. Countless courageous adventurers embarked on tremendous explorations with thousands of navigational errors to turn that flat world into the round one that we enjoy and travel today.

What part of your world is still flat? What part of your world is still trapped in old patterns of ignorance?

Human beings have a few fundamental requirements known as Commons. These are the resources that are common and essential to life. They are earth, water and air for all life, and one other particularly essential to human life. Humans require freedom in order to develop hope; to set and establish their visions and perform the daily tasks in alignment with their dreams. Commons — including freedom — are essential to human life and are therefore sacred as a birthright.

Expanding human paradigms beyond the limitations of old fears requires the same enthusiastic explorations that turned the flat world round. How do you achieve this freedom and adventure in your world on a daily basis? How do you take charge of and enable your dreams by insuring that they can be accomplished with your skillset. Where do you step off the edge of the horizon — beyond the limits of old established fears - and sail forth into the lands of your inspirations?

See to it that you exercise this impulse daily. See to it that you draw new maps of your world often. See to it that you are the captain of you own ship. See to it that you cherish the Commons and exercise the Freedom that you were born to have. See to it that your world is round.

NOTES TO MY ANGELS:

24

In the reality of our Quantum life on Earth, observation is everything . . . in an immeasurable instant, observation creates the experience you are having right before your senses and all without your conscious awareness. It is known as maya — the grand illusion — and it must be mastered in order to pass on to the next level of consciousness.

Life's greatest purpose and opportunity is to master the code behind this illusion and snap the "leash" that binds you to its mystery. To master this is to first become aware that your observation is creating your experience — everything that happens to you is in fact your responsibility. Next, trust this awareness you are having of the infinite responsibility of your possibility. Lastly, trust yourself to experience the experience that arrives at your door . . . knowing you never receive more than you can handle, or different than you expect. It is all about awareness.

When this all takes place in each moment without effort; you trust yourself without reservation. Now you will spend your life running "off leash" to create and recreate your reality as you would consciously choose. In this state you live each moment for what it is and pass joyfully through these moments, retaining all the blessings and releasing the debris.

This is known as liberation!

NOTES TO MY ANGELS:

ASPECT THREE

Experience
the
Experience

ASPECT THREE
— Experience the Experience —

25

As both Guru Nanak and Lord Buddha said so many centuries ago; life is either a balanced experience or an imbalanced experience, but both take place on the stage of this world's perfect balance. The blessing or the curse of the human experience is not with the world, but in the perception of the experience of the world. Other than that, this world is actually perfectly aligned — known to science as the material balance-point. The entire eco-system thrives on it.

Science also tells us that stress, friction, pressure and tension are the universal bonding forces of this world; they create this material balance-point. They exist everywhere, holding this world together. Without them, there could be no physical reality . . . it would simply disintegrate into a chaos of random particles.

When you suffer from one or more of these four bonding forces (you feel pressured, or stressed, or tension or friction), there is either an imbalance in — your expression, or your projection, or your perception. You will experience the pressure, tension, stress and friction in every situation when you are outside their balance-point. Since they are always present, experiencing them indicates a misconception or mis-perception of their perfectly balanced presence.

In order to bring your experience back to their point of balance, you must perform the inner work where your perception begins. Inner work has no immediate measurable reward; it is only through your projected actions that you are certain it will bear fruit.

Without instant gratification, there is little emotional attraction to meditating, or chanting, or stretching into the body-glove with yoga. It takes effort to achieve the results and the results are definitely not instant. If you do these practices however, you will find that the perceived imbalances will re-balance. You will begin to experience the world within you and around you as if pressure, tension, stress and friction do not even exist.

This is the material balance-point . . . this creates Heaven on Earth. This will become the common experience within the new evolution of human consciousness . . . this is the greatest possibility of life on purpose.

NOTES TO MY ANGELS:

26

When you form an impression, your system dedicates its entire perception to substantiating this exact view. The senses become selective with what they register in order to achieve this certainty. This is an ancient survival tactic . . . "safety" . . . achieved via always being right. In today's evolutionary phase - by virtue of this neurotic survival mechanism - the deep subconscious mostly prefers being right to being happy. The reward system in our education facilities pounds this into our children's psyche, year after year after year.

We all have this core instability; it is an evolutionary sensation on which all other feelings are built. When the cover sensations become too numerous over time, this core sense is heavily distorted and masked. Your feelings become inaccurate, but you insist on certainty within the illusion and grasp for more illusion to increase this false certainty. Thus, the roots of greed and obsession begin to dominate. This is the 21st century and it is destroying the planet.

It is now time to move from this ignorance of the false known — to the wisdom of embracing the vast unknown. The long and winding road of physical evolution eventually returns home where our physical machine of work (our human body) becomes a refined instrument of worship. The next evolutionary phase will now take this instrument of worship and tune it to its highest harmonic frequency. Old attitudes and impressions - caught within your senses for ages - will become meaningless. This will be frightening and many in society will react with rage. Lend your time to gently accomplishing this goal within your self and around your community. Never eat alone . . . associate with those who have your back.

When you cease seeing the objects in space and begin to perceive the oneness of place, the majority of your survival mechanism disappears. This requires more courage than urge. Gently, the connection between yourself and all else appears as if it was always there. This connectedness (for example) displays and perceives the branches and leaves of a tree - not as branches and leaves - but as tree. You begin to see the truth of what is . . . not what appears to be. This is freedom . . . this is liberation. This will ultimately be the saving grace of humanity, but it will be resisted . . . so be gentle.

NOTES TO MY ANGELS: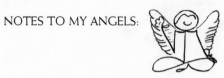

27

We identify the experience of our existence through the interpretation of our observations. We then register this interpretation to memory, as a conclusion and store it away for a future response. This cycle repeats over and over with new interpretations of new observations with new responses waiting for the next moment.

All of this is stored and recalled, while we live as an identity of an opinion of our experience of the observation of our experience within our existence. WOW . . . we use these observations, interpretations and memories to shape our view. We relate to the 'world' around us with this view. We shape every response and reaction that we have, and we do it with these exact tools. This defines our purpose, our process, our preferences . . . and on and on . . . Eventually all the memory, and further anticipation produced by this memory, begins to override the accuracy of our observations . . . we ultimately completely misread what is happening. But we cannot be convinced of this in the slightest.

We are constantly moving from the presentation of all this information — which is the present moment — into our interpretation which is the past — and our projection — which is the future . . . we move from presentation into interpretation into projection. Our presentation is measured as the finite potential (physical world) and our projection is measured as the infinitely possible (mental world) . . . our presentation is measured as space and our projection is experienced as time.

Out of all this there are very few components you can manage, and then master, where the mixtures and ratios determine the quality of your life. How to interpret your observations is one part you can manage and another is the ratio between how much of the 'infinitely possible' (hope, purpose and vision) you employ within your 'finite potential' (the physical realities of the observed). The more 'infinitely possible' you use in this mix, the more push back and unpredictable adventure you receive. The more 'finite potential' you use, the less push back and the more safety and predictability you receive.

Remember: in this particular instance — safety can ultimately become dangerous because safety can bring stagnation, then stagnation brings frustration leading to emotional outbursts. If you prefer fulfillment . . . mix your life moderately—not enormously—in favor of adventure . . . you will be rewarded with gentle, graceful and unexplained joys as you progress consistently toward mastery.

NOTES TO MY ANGELS:

28

The breath is the voice of the Soul - the heartbeat is the Taal (the sacred rhythms) . . . the combination of these two, sing the songs of life. It is said by the mystics that destiny is written on our foreheads — this is the screen projected from the frontal lobe of the brain . . . seat of the highest frequencies of the collective human consciousness.

Every human has a statement to make with their life, a status to have from their life, a state to be in during life. As long as this song is playing, these requirements are actively engaged. When this song plays from the highest consciousness of courage, you become a seeker . . . consciously, actively and tirelessly seeking . . . you are a student of the Cosmos. When you do not allow this song to play in your heart — you are a window shopper, perhaps claiming to be a seeker, but you are not seeking. You are playing it safe.

When we face any dilemma, the Cosmos has already composed the corrections. The only question that remains is: which side of this event will you take your stand on — the dilemma or the correction . . . the confusion or the commitment . . . the shopper or the seeker.

Living in these current times builds up a great deal of emotional and mental shopper's "noise." This is a weakening process that robs us of our innate human powers. One way to respond to this and create the graceful state of a quiet mind of dynamic silence — a mind that can think and create solutions — is to breathe part of each day with what is called 'breath of fire'. This is pumping the belly in on each exhale and out on each inhale. Do this with a steady breathing rhythm of about 80 to 90 breaths per minute. Do this, while sitting in easy pose or a chair, for 3 minutes several times each day.

Let the voice of the Soul sing the song of your life and turn you into the seeker you were born to be in this life.

NOTES TO MY ANGELS:

29

Perception was the first moment of creation — in fact it was the cause — the desire to reflect upon the self. It began as a mirror, longing to belong to its reflection . . . the self, to the self. Since longing and belonging are one in the same, no witness existed before this first moment. An illusion was required to create the definition of creation. Life, an intangible without a witness, needed to be learned . . . needed to be experienced through learned perceptions. The food of experience desired the senses and the sensations to be appreciated . . . life required living.

Once the taste of life was learned, this experience became attached to the senses. The task of liberation is the unlearning of this attachment to the senses. When our senses are ignored, we might transcend some parts of time, but we still fear the death required to pass through the gates of this illusion that is guarding the spiritual plane. We spend lifetimes as a prisoner in this fear, coming and going, going and coming — trial and failure upon trial and error. The concept of life has become designed around these trials — these are called the lessons of living — these errors have become our lifestyles.

The ultimate lesson of life — the final stage of our trial — is to know beyond mere knowing that there is no such thing as death. We continue the cycle — to come and go over lifetimes — until this lesson has been mastered. Once mastered, fear dissolves into fearlessness and the entire Cosmos becomes our cozy home. When the entire Cosmos is home, there is no space beyond this comfort. When there is no uncomfortable space, there is no uncomfortable time . . . not even the unknown future is uncomfortable. When there is no discomfort, there is no separation and that first moment of perception is undone . . . the senses detached . . . the witness dismissed . . . the perception dismantled.

Longing disappears into a perfect partnership — a perfect marriage — consciousness becomes bonded to the soul rather than to the body . . . no witness, no longing, no perception, no separation . . . AKAL . . . deathlessness prevails everywhere. The completion of the illusion (Maya) is complete . . . I am one.

NOTES TO MY ANGELS:

30

When eighty-five to ninety-five percent of your world is currently dedicated to the affairs of your body — and the pathway to happiness requires this attention to be divided evenly between body, mind and spirit —the solution to happiness becomes excitingly self-evident. Create the balance in your world so that the outcome is clear.

Everyone has one-hundred percent of their own time . . . everyone knows what evenly distributing this time and attention would mean. This means everyone who lives in the world of freedoms. Therefore, everyone living in the world of freedoms is able to experience happiness. It requires that a choice be made and then this choice is to be disciplined. For those who live in a world of slavery, totalitarian rule or extreme hardship this is not possible. For those of you who live in freedom and are still not applying the requirements to happiness; think of what you are throwing away.

Observe this truism without fear and without wanting it to be different. Observe it without offense, without defense, without preference. In this way you will observe exactly what it is . . . the answer to your dreams . . . not negotiating through opinions that have been filtered with unnecessary perceptions. Seeing it as it is . . .

In this light, you can observe a pathway that has never been clear to you before. The power of this experience teaches you how to distribute your attention evenly between body, mind and spirit and mark the path to happiness. This even distribution transcends time-space and heals the impossible . . . understands the undeniable . . . achieves the improbable and manifests happiness everywhere . . . the greatest opportunities pop up in your life out of the 'Blue'. Let us cherish the freedoms we do have and work to discipline our balance within them. Then let us campaign for these freedoms to be evenly distributed around this planet because remember: happiness is a human birthright . . . not a privilege.

NOTES TO MY ANGELS:

31

The Buddha was exact in his praise of the middle path, the path of moderation. He stressed this path because, as he said, we are in fact standing at the absolute middle of creation anyway. We always reside (in consciousness) halfway between the micro-world within us and the macro-world outside. Everyone sits in the exact center of the self . . . becoming consciously aware of this position is the purpose of a daily practice (sadhana).

Guru Nanak was speaking to the same point when [in Japji] he expresses — "There are worlds upon worlds . . . universes upon universes . . . existences upon existences."

The universe is only a slice of the far larger multiverse . . . this too, only a section of the infinite Cosmos, including the entire zero-mass of infinity's void. This infinite zero-mass is the Gu from which the Ru of light/matter is born . . . hence the origins of the Sanskrit word Guru - (bringing light from the infinite darkness).

As you become more conscientious of your place at this center-point — the point between your inner-sphere and the outer-sphere — your true-identity begins to intrigue you. A phenomenon occurs during such a sensation; it delivers an absolute sense of being one with nature. Balancing this true-identity — establishing a clear self-image in the world's ever-challenging environment of stress, friction, pressure and tension — is a key to health, prosperity and the success of all relationships.

Every human in this multiverse wants to climb his or her "Mountain" . . . wants to achieve a dream that matches this character and caliber of the self-image. One of the best exercises for such an effort is the effortless, silent contemplation on the sensation of breathing . . . the sensation of being breath, rather than being the breather of the breath. This is a deduction, not a production — this is introspection, not projection — this is an inaction that reveals the middle pathway to your "Mountain top" . . . the world of your fulfillment.

Remember: you can always see the Mountain of your dreams from a greater distance, but when you get up to the base camp — ready to climb and do the work and fulfill this dream — all you can see are the foothills (the problems) directly in front of you . . . the challenges that surround you. "You cannot see the forest for the trees." You must climb over these foothills — over all these challenges — with great trust that the "Mountain" is there . . . it is coming on its way toward you. This is the essence of the story of Mohamed and the mountain.

Use a conscious breathing exercise (pranayam) to tune into and experience the essence of each step — this is the middle path; this is the way of ultimately being at ease with your "Mountain" . . . being at ease with the greatest possibilities of your life.

NOTES TO MY ANGELS:

32

When in any particular moment or period of your life — a moment where dynamic growth, for any reason, has just occurred — the lack of all those old familiar fittings with their patterns nestled neatly together into your familiar environment — this lack will cause considerable angst. Fitting back into the older patterns requires a refusal to accommodate your new growth. This is very common and is the reason that true growth is so difficult. This refusal and then reversal of growth will instantly take place through the 'groping' for the familiarity of old environments. You are then left wondering what has gone wrong . . . while, at the same time, definitely relieved that you are back to "normal."

If, on the other hand, you allow this angst to simply state its case of uncertainty without accommodating or reacting to it — you then relax all resistance to the unfamiliar — the new growth will find its new patterns in your new environment and ultimately become your new familiarity. This requires courage and is the only way to sustain growth.

In other words . . . don't try to fit in . . . you fit perfectly in you. By allowing the discomfort of not fitting in to simply be what it is; the arena around you is forced to comply with and verify your new form. In addition to courage, this requires tremendous quantities of faith and trust. It is not easy . . . it is ultimately extremely rewarding . . . it is extremely abnormal. If your need is to be normal then you will not walk on this path.

Remember: the only constant in this universe is change . . . so as Gandhi once said, "Become the change you want to see."

NOTES TO MY ANGELS:

33

Think of the fact that the main purpose in life is to actually experience the experience you are having; to live the life you are living and comprehend all of the sensations that are taking place — all of the signals and all of the clues — using all of the biological, experiential, visceral, emotional and psychological capacities. This is a long way off from what we are doing in this world at this moment in time.

But, we are entering into an era of re-evolution where all the limited horizons, the restricted views, the simpler explanations that have served us in the past will no longer be sufficient to move us forward. We cannot go about life remaining in a safe zone — viewing the world and experiencing it through the same old filters. These ways we have always known will continue the same predictable ups and downs and the familiarity will give us the illusion of safety. But we have reached the end of this road and this is becoming ever more obvious.

Life is inviting us to take this moment in time — to engage a brand new opportunity — to take a risk that has never been taken — to initiate the process of altering our perceptions and seeing how all things actually are. We are to begin the elimination of all the familiar filters, the ones that only show us what we already know. We are to take this moment and learn something new from the broader horizons and expanded views of the infinite multi-verse. We are to build a new set of explanations to account for what we are already experiencing. This is the time that is upon us. The old ways are tired and worn out.

This is in fact opening up to the new stage of our evolution . . . expanding conscious awareness. Every specie in the past that refused this opportunity have disappeared into extinction. What a great opportunity to break that old mold. What a wonderful moment to build on life's endless experiences. What a powerful idea to renew our purpose and then live on purpose. What a great new day to have a great day . . . the world is waiting . . . the universe is changing . . . become who you want to become.

NOTES TO MY ANGELS:

34

When you are no longer the witness; when you are no longer holding out for a peek to see if you are 'OK' . . . you are in that moment — 'OK' — to the 'nth' degree. Unaware of all that you might 'not' be; you are simply employing life-force (Prana) as a means of being who you are. The perfect mantra for this condition is: I am who I am . . . that is that.

All that you are becomes merely what you are. All that you are engaged in becomes simply engaged. You are experiencing the experience without the need for a witness to witness the experience. You do not require anything to justify you, or verify you, or confirm anything other than the experience of your existence.

This is what yogis call a state of grace . . . it can come from having complete confidence; it can come from extreme simplicity or it can come from deep trust. The word confidence is from the Latin and 'con' means — with — and 'fidence' means — faith. Faith is a subject that has no object. It is never faith in something (that would be reliance) it is simple; it is just faith.

This confidence allows for many things including — the experience of life to be that of living the experience. It is when you have the experience of joy without needing an explanation of a reason; or when you experience love and require no justification for the experience. You thereby disallow any doubts from becoming the witness to your experience and there is then no disruption to the joy of your love. This is the pure existence having a pure experience. This is known in Sanskrit as 'Khalsa'.

The further you move from this purity of being and into the need for a witness, or to be witnessed; the more you must justify and the more you must employ the intellect to explain what you are experiencing. You are then not living the experience of life; you are witnessing a concept of life. This will naturally and eventually turn into pain and the purpose of life then becomes the avoidance of this pain. We have been involved with this dilemma for many thousands of years. It is life based on conclusions drawn from bias (the angles of perception). Life has become a struggle to reduce this pain, to engage in alternative witnessing. Life has become the filling of time with the explanations of the justifications of the condemnations of the pain.

Life becomes "unsafe" in this myriad of actions, distractions and reactions. Purpose becomes the need to guarantee safety . . . an unfulfilled and unfulfillable constant companion. In this endless cycle of pain to pleasure — pleasure to pain, the emphasis searches for a witness to witness the experience that is not being experienced. The riddle is unsolvable.

Your task is to cast this cycle into a black-hole. Every galaxy has one. Dive into the experience of your experience and become the Soul having a human experience while being humane. Be the experience itself and your birthright of happiness will appear as if it were there all along. Because it has been . . . it is the cosmic law of time-space . . . it is the nature of nature. Happiness is the experience of life — experiencing life.

Have you not had those moments — sensed the faint sense of these hints of deep happiness within the glimpses of your experience? They come when you have allowed yourself to experience any experience from within the innocence of your faint, but insistent courage? This is the true you being the pure experience! This is you being Khalsa.

NOTES TO MY ANGELS:

35

As humans we actually believe that when we move from one place to another place to another place, we are having the experiences of each place and that the places are different. However, the realities of the majority of the experiences that we have are actually traveling with us. This is in what is known as 'Place' ('capitalized' for distinction) in the science of Humanology. You enter a space, but 'Place' travels with you — it is yours and it defines the majority of your experience.

Place is, in fact, a complex equation carried within the electro-magnetic field that surrounds you . . . known as the Aura. This is a filter of your input and output. It is constructed by four facets of your human being. These are your Feelings, Perceptions, Pace and Place . . . each one constructed interactively over tremendous amounts of time . . . even generations biologically . . . even incarnations cosmologically.

As you move from the traffic on a road to the quiet of a room you have changed the space of your experience, but you have carried within you, the definitions of the experience that you will be experiencing. The inner noise (the definitions) traveling with you into the quiet room is far more present than your environmental shift. You will continue to experience the inner sensations of the noisy traffic you left outside until they fade from your memory or are replaced. In order to change the foundation of 'Place', you must transform the inner 'codes' . . . you must work on the inner constructs of your Feelings, the inner constructs of your Perceptions, and the inner constructs of your Pacing.

Simply changing the space (the persons, the locations and the things) with which and within which you exist will change very little . . . 'Place' is only slightly modified by these external changes. Space is merely the setting in which you experience your experience; your Feelings, Perceptions and Pace define this experience. 'Place' will manifest based on your propensity to Feel, to Perceive and to Pace. Changing this 'Place' — which you carry with you — affects the entire experience of your experience . . . affects the entire sense of your existence . . . affects your entire outlook and your outcomes. 'Place' is the experience and the experiencer.

Do not try to understand this by using your thoughts . . . allow it to sink into your body and your being. Allow it to contribute to your Place.

"The observer and the observed are one . . . they are in fact the same event."
Guru Nanak - India (ad.1489) "The observer defines the observed" Albert
Einstein - (ad. 1909)

NOTES TO MY ANGELS:

ASPECT FOUR

Commitment

ASPECT FOUR
— Commitment —

36

When you are young and bright and aiming your entire life toward hopes and dreams with all the possible power, there are few thoughts that this will ever change. There are also very few thoughts that the illusion of time passing will have diminishing affects upon your life. Then — without the consciousness acknowledging it — years pass, decades pass, the illusion of the time of your life passes. In doing so, it poses the question. Are you closer to the aims of your youth, or are you a copy of a copy, a tangent of a tangent, a limit of a limitation? Are you an imitation of your intended path?

If the answer is not . . . " I AM — WHO I AM — THAT IS THAT ! " . . . then the answer resides in your sea of pain. Conscious of it or not, numb to it or not . . . it is still painful in the long run.

The key to remaining powerful and on point - the key to living in the answer of; "I AM — WHO I AM" is a combination of avid flexibility and daily consistency. Flexibility allows you to take no offense to the constant offense of time. Consistency allows you to successfully navigate through the constant defensive nature of space . . . for every one of your actions it gives you an equal reaction. You must consistently and flexibly check your course against a "master-map" in order for your life to remain connected with the direction of your core intention. Otherwise, it is increasingly easy to become that tangent of a tangent and then a copy of a copy and then the limits of the limitations of your imitations.

The evidence is in; you are either moving forward or backward, but life is never stagnant . . . change is the only real constant. There is no standing still in this material creation. Therefore, one must apply a strong daily directional intent to remain on point throughout time . . . otherwise; your direction will be chosen for you - not by you.

When you appear to stand still in doubt, confusion, or fear; you are actually moving — just not in any direction of your choosing. You are being shifted

onto the tangents that streak throughout timespace . . . at someone else's pace
. . . toward someone else's place. You are living someone else's dream. This is
the danger-zone infiltrating your "safety" zone of indecision, doubt, fear,
confusion and inaction.

All the 'shoulds' and the 'coulds' are great indicators — but time-space
requires your active participation. Accomplishment only takes place when you
actively participate with your intentions. Therefore, fully commit to participate
in the dreams of your choice and do so against all the risks confronting you.

Further: learn the living art of the martial arts — become responsive to the
defensive offensiveness of this material world without taking offense, without
being offensive or defensive. Leave no track-backs in the fabric of space and
time will not knock you down in its defection from, or its reaction to your projection.

Make this your daily occurrence — 'flexible consistency . . . persistently
affirming your goals'. Experience the living affirmations of being YOU every
day. Do not wish upon time from the sidelines of life, but commit full
participation in the actual — active — construction of your goals. Retrieve all
the dreams that you knew in your youth, or if you are still young, never leave
them . . . become their guarantee [daily] and you will live them. This is
spiritual growth in the new evolution of human consciousness.

NOTES TO MY ANGELS:

37

To be consistently growing in the midst of life's changes, charges and challenges, we must constantly check with ourselves: "am I committed to being right, or am I committed to feeling good, or am I committed to growing?" Then remember, growth does not always feel good, and feeling good does not always provide growth, and neither one is going to always be considered "right" by the rest.

There must always be a balanced conscious coordination between the sensations of your emotional and physical worlds, and the sensibilities of your evolutionary progress through this world. The physical and emotional bodies speak in a temporal language of selfishness . . . a drive to comfort and pleasure . . . a primitive means of survival that desires being right — first and foremost. This is not a bad thing, if it is not the only thing, but it should never be more than one third of your life's focus. The mind's conscious expansion and your spiritual fulfillment are to balance out the other two thirds of your purpose.

A baby is completely body centric, but as we grow, we are supposed to balance this out. Are you growing? There is an old saying in yoga about this: "Everybody grows old, but very few grow up."

Without releasing the shackles of this body centric need — which honors feelings over growth — you will be forever dancing to the uncommitted beat that progresses only part way toward your goals. We call this the "halfway-dance" and it takes place in the "comfort lounge" on the "first floor" of your "halfway house." It is in fact, a sub-primitive human nature — it arrived with the conceptual mind around one hundred thousand years ago and has been developing and taking command ever since.

Without engaging the primitive drive to survive, or the exalted drive to grow, commitment cannot engage and the pain from lacking fulfillment becomes life's entire focus. Everything 'halfway' becomes the theme . . . the perfected obsessions of life. Civilization supports this theme in order to maintain the illusion of 'safe concepts replacing dangerous experiences'. This is why today's youth are into extremes (sports, clothes, tattoos, piercing, video games, etc.); they are in search of the real experience in a world obsessed and driven by false images and meaningless concepts.

The halfway dance has been mastered and marketed over the past two hundred years. It dances for all who pay it attention and anyone who pays the fee. Life has become about earning a living, rather than living and experiencing the life already earned. Image has become more important than connection and with this — the concept out-plays the content. The halfway "market" fills with participants who are making a killer living on this halfway dance, but never really living [as alive, ecstatic and conscious beings]. Fear has become the feeling of guidance because separation always requires a sense of safety no matter how false. This "safe-zone" has become the most dangerous place to live . . . especially when you die in it as a completely unfulfilled human.

It is time to turn over the leaf . . . live in the risk of total commitment. It is not about the mirror's reflection being right (the image); it is about the projection being you (the fulfillment).

Make this your routine on a daily basis — look into a mirror and challenge yourself to be YOU and nothing less. Smile and be vocal in this exercise . . . this may start out very serious, but it will soon turn joyful. You will find yourself in front of your SELF, standing at the mirror on the edge of each morning, grateful for a relationship that has become extremely REAL . . . from one that was assumed and granted.

Then take this real-time relationship into the field of your life . . . out into the risk of your commitment. Reproduce it with tremendous enthusiasm for the greatest possibilities of your life.

NOTES TO MY ANGELS:

38

The healing property of medicinal plants has evolved over the millennia using micro-steps as a means of protecting the plant from its outside invaders. These little steps of incremental protection allow the plant to avoid a total invasion. However, since every action has an equal reaction — if these moves of cure were too large or too fast, the reaction to the cure would be equally severe. This would set up a rollercoaster of chaos that would be very difficult — perhaps impossible — for evolution to manage. These are the reactions, called side effects in modern medicine that work far too fast and extreme. This is not natural and will eventually have to correct.

All the events we pass through in life are an exact, elaborately calculated cosmic sequence of our life's lessons. As humans, we are repeatedly challenged through the logic of time passing, to become our own cure. Taking a lesson from these medicinal plants in naturopathy, we must begin using such incremental steps to reduce the push back against our cures. Create and build in little steps; do not ask for bombs to hit, explosions are not constructive. Construction arrives by accepting that there are no exceptions to the cosmic balance of action and reaction.

The additional alchemy of this human reality is — when a cure takes place in one of us, it is then available to all of us. Read — The Hundredth Monkey, by Ken Keyes Jr.

The only question remains: can this cosmic principle hold our attention and produce enough movement through our surrender to avoid the frustration of boredom? Until we accept graduation to the next level via surrender, we will fail in many of our endeavors with resistance. By working without resistance and frustration, the little steps eventually add up to success. This is why herbal alchemy is so effective, little steps adding together where big steps would break down from big opposition.

Resistance is the thief — surrender is the gift giver. Resistance robs vitality that is required to overcome complexities. By surrendering through these complexities in small unnoticeable increments, we discover an open pathway ... the very route of natural and naturopathic healing.

NOTES TO MY ANGELS: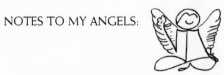

39

The passage of time is like an hourglass where the grains of sand are moments passing through the narrows of the present moment . . . this narrows known (in time) as "now." Sand that has fallen through this narrows is called the "past" and the sand waiting to fall is called the "future." However, remember, there is a view of the glass of time that can see it all in a single glance.

Spiritual mastery — and now scientific study — shows us that time is an illusion; it is a limited perception contained and constrained within our five senses. Past and future are pure imagination, yet extremely convenient markers. They allow us to keep track of all our concepts by making the order of 'things' more logical. Our five senses produce a logical view of the world and this view emulates the "passage of time."

There is a more advanced way to view the cosmos; one that sees all time together as one. In this view — the past, the present and the future are all just the sand in the glass with no reference to its movement. This view, known as the continuum, is the power of our intuition, premonition and the various psychic abilities. Instead of watching each moment of the sand as it moves in the moment, it focuses on all of the sand at once, and just as with all of time ... all of the sand is in fact . . . always existing.

Every human has this inherent capacity to perceive and interpret time in this way, but most have not yet activated the "equipment." The world at large discredits such attempts to engage this view by branding it as weird, crazy, or dreaming. This way of viewing life and the world is a human skill that can be activated and highly trained.

Commitment is one of the most powerful tools in your human inventory. It overrides impulse and places control of your experience back in your hands. Commitment is one of the many pathways to the power of intuition; a perfect way to embrace and comprehend the 'passage of time' to guide your life toward your goals.

An extremely practical method of discovering, strengthening and tuning up your commitment is through yoga, meditation and chanting. Kundalini yoga stretches you into your body glove to remove the emotional distractions and physical discomforts. Meditation and chanting clear the brain of its chatter (conscious and unconscious) and enable clarity to flourish. Tuning this human instrument on a regular, consistent, daily basis presents you with the joy of knowing that you actually know. This is at the very root of the power of intuition.

NOTES TO MY ANGELS:

40

When a man commits to a position . . . occupying no dimension . . . projecting limitlessly forever . . . this is a liberated man. When a woman trusts the imagination of her total vision . . . agreeing to her limitlessly forever . . . this is a liberated woman.

When these are united — the man and the woman — the man and the man — the woman and the woman — the student and the teacher — all relate within what is known as love . . . no limiting conditional time-lines, no limits to the dimensions, no limits to the trust of possibilities, no limits to the imagination.

Within this sacred geometry of oneness, as all the pre-scripts and the post-scripts are relaxed, the options multiply through the outcomes and discovery becomes gold amongst the dirt. By not living by the rule of others, you respect yourself . . . by not condemning the attempts of others to rule, you respect their self. All is — in fact —the one self, for there is not — in fact — any 'other'.

Liberation is never from anything, it is always toward everything. The history of its path [the 'from'] can be either (because of) or (in spite of) . . . the trajectory of its path [toward] is always the commitment from within, or the trusting of within. This actually disables the 'without' to control anything.

Let this 'maze' sit within you — without your brain trying to put the puzzle together. This is one for the heart to assemble with its steady loving rhythms. The heart has the deposit of your cosmology to work from, and is able to perceive through this 'maze' into the lens of infinity.

Let it do its job, . . . it will always do it well . . . it is 'amazing' that way. Such a Heaven on Earth will become the common experience in the New Evolution.

NOTES TO MY ANGELS:

41

Every human being has the opportunity to be one of three personas in life: a 'Placeholder'; an 'Experiencer'; or a 'Phenomenon'.

A 'Placeholder' remains on the same page of the book of life throughout the days, weeks, months and years and specializes in this stasis masquerading as stability. Called conservative, it attempts to conserve what already is . . . fearful of most growth into areas that are new. It claims that it desires change, but it does not want it to be different. A Placeholder also maintains the stagnation where fearfulness gathers.

An 'Experiencer' emphasizes writing new chapters in the book of life; working with the new, but ever mindful of the shoreline and rarely moving out too far beyond the horizon. There is a sense of adventure with an experience of growth and this is a good thing. An 'Experiencer' will write brand new chapters as the life gently progresses and there is very little stagnation.

Being a 'Phenomenon' is a rare opportunity to use your wings of absolute relentless courage. A 'Phenomenon' will constantly write new chapters and even produce an entirely new book. When a person has this special ability to write a new book, they are one in a million. They bring about a 'quickening' - advancing evolution itself. Our history is filled with tales of such quickenings . . . when the path of evolution takes a profound leap forward they form the core of the renaissance. Those who bring these about are rarely - if ever - accepted during their lifetime. This wholesale rejection tends to discourage these actions, for this becomes a lonely and challenging path. The only way to cover this challenge is that the phenomenal person creates a strong relationship with the center of the Cosmos.

This is what we need to change in this new era of the new evolution . . . we must publically recognize the outrageous beauty of our phenomenal brothers and sisters who have this much courage. We must be flexible to accept them and do so while they are alive. We must welcome their enormous leap of faith and limitless growth while it is happening.

And further: we must courageously ignite this tendency within ourselves. Every one of us has the power to turn our lives into a source of phenomenon.

Now is a time; Earth requires this great change — bless you today with this courageous effort for tomorrow — bless you today for with the evolution of human consciousness . . . bless you today . . .

NOTES TO MY ANGELS:

42

"The best laid plans of..." "The road to hell is paved with..." "Money is the root of . . ." All these prominent one-liners state the same fact; any strong intention will consistently receive strong resistance. This is the physical dynamics of life . . . of our world . . . of this universe. "For every action there is equal reaction."

This resistance can seem offensive and rude . . . it can seem personal and punishing. Do not turn it into this kind of monster; do not take offense to the offensiveness that refuses to accept your intention . . . your will. This is the barometer on the dashboard of your life . . . merely the universe acting in accordance with the laws of nature. Your job is to master the navigation of these laws.

All of the acceptance and understanding that you require to navigate this resistance is contained within the origination of your intention itself. This is the engine; it allows you to start dreaming it . . . to dare to express it . . . to attempt to manifest it in the first place. You must acknowledge that surrounding every intention is a collection of great reasons for every ounce of this natural resistance. It delivers the exercise to strengthen the intention to survive. It delivers the dynamic shaping for it to move forward. It is like the shell to the baby bird . . . the strength to survive comes with the action of breaking out. The definition of the bird itself is contained within its persistence and resistance. No one dares to help the baby bird escape, for if they did . . . guaranteed it would perish.

It is like the saying: "When you are going through hell, keep going!" Just understand that resistance is the natural action prescribed against you to manifest your strength. The last thing that you want to do; the last thing you can afford to do, is interpret this resistance as a personal attack of ill intention. It is not; it is a perfect attack and it defines the magnitude and greatness of your intention. Remember: "You can judge your strength by the strength of your enemy."

NOTES TO MY ANGELS:

43

Freedom is a human requirement; it allows you to live your life as a mission — not an omission — not requiring permission. This freedom is essential to the fulfillment of your life's purpose.

Freedom will manifest either your greatest dreams or your worst nightmares . . . whichever one you place the most free energy. The energy of thought receives its direction from the amount of trust you place in yourself, your world, your universe, and the path of destiny you are walking on.

When your thoughts are bound up by fear, you make nightmares your reality . . . you become a slave to the world of fear. Even then, freedom is essential to your evolution. The gift of freewill must be free; for even when you have manifested these nightmares, you must have the right and the opportunity to learn from them . . . then create your dreams from the new experience.

All other creatures perish from these mistakes — humans learn from them. When there is freedom — it does not matter if the wind is blowing with you, or against you. You are free to make as many choices . . . free to make as many mistakes . . . free to take as much time as it will take you to get it right.

Even when the wind is blowing hard against you, you still have the capacity to guide your life on a path that will eventually arrive at your destination. This freedom is an extremely sacred trust and must be trusted; for freedom creates the liberated view that even harsh opposition is workable.

Become an advocate of this freedom by putting it to great use in your world. Become an advocate of this freedom by allowing others to make up their own choices even when they are quite contrary to yours. Become an advocate of this freedom and create a world that works for all of us.

NOTES TO MY ANGELS:

ASPECT FIVE

Yoga
Anatomy

ASPECT FIVE
—Yoga Anatomy—

44

Ayurveda — the oldest health science on Earth — has eight branches . . . Rasayana is one of them. Ayurveda ('ayur' is 'science' and 'veda' is 'life') deals with measuring, transforming and revitalizing all of the inner energies that sustain a healthy life. Rasayana works with the most vital of these energies. 'Rasa' is essence and 'ayana' is the path . . . rasayana - path of our essence.

Self checking and correcting at this vital level was a daily practice for the ancient yogis of 'Humanitaria' (the geographical area now containing Persia, India, and Burma). This practice maintained their perfect health into very old age . . . as a matter of fact there was only slight aging even when living past 100 years.

Checking on ones vitality has been completely lost in today's obsessive pursuit of objects, resources and concepts. The game — in the "modern" world — has become dedicated to feeding the body and the intellect and accomplishing their many goals of external measure. In fact we are not living within an experience of life; we are living within an empty bubble, an intellectual concept of life. We are not connecting to our essence at all anymore. We are not on a path of happiness; we are on a path of disruption, disease, disappointment and distrust. This madness is craving our vitality like a parasite . . . it pursues a highly developed and complex misconception of value. We have lost our inner-sense, the infinite nature of innocence. We have lost true value.

Now is the time to make the move and counter this obsession that measures value through accumulation. We are not the squirrels or the crows that must line our nests; we are the humans who have a responsibility to experience and share the essence of this experience with all others. We are the humans who — if we use our system properly — are capable of appreciating the pure joy that comes with this essence.

We are the stewards of life; let us actually begin to live as such. 'Hu' means light and 'man' means mind. Let us use this power of the mind and shed its light on every circumstance. Let us derive the most prosperous outcome from each moment. This is the role of a steward.

This is rasa-ayana . . . this is the path of pure essence . . . this is the true value of human existence. This is the angle that meets and triangulates 'nature's law' — "that for every action there is an equal reaction" — and turns this law into the fruition of compassion and cooperation, not competition and destruction.

This is your role; this is your opportunity as a person of consciousness . . . it is high time to live in it.

NOTES TO MY ANGELS:

45

The body is an extremely sacred vessel . . . but it is not you. The body is a living gift, a complex instrument of functions and sensations with an excellent capacity to connect through worship . . . but it is not you.

Today the body is confused with image. Our modern economy preys on this confusion and relegates the body to an empty physical mechanism that displays this needy image. It beckons us to purchase in order to ease our pain and insecurity . . . but it is all a perfect set up . . . obsession with image stimulates the economy, but it never stimulates the human harmony. Quite the opposite . . . it fixates on competition and creates pain out of the ensuing battles.

The modern industrial economy has relegated the body to a position of burden, a pack animal that carries the brain and the stomach and the image through life. When the body is limited to this role, life and living have been replaced by a concept of life and a concept of living . . . it all seems quite empty. This is what humanity has been developing over these decades with power marketing. It has been called progress, but it is in need of progressive transformation right now.

The body is a sacred gift, endowed to carry consciousness through a human experience. Simply stated, your body is a transceiver; you transmit a physical image out as physical light — it reflects off everything around you and returns as your environment. With this reflection delivered to your body's senses; you can either fixate on how you feel, which is life's concept, or you can have an experience of the feeling and find the lesson within it . . . which is living. When the body focuses on image, concept becomes the controlling factor and image becomes the super high maintenance insecurity.

It is time to nourish a more conscious, more fulfilling journey . . . the actual experience of the experience of life.

There is a pre-verbal mindset connecting beyond image and there is a post-verbal mindset correlating with image — ultimately, both are important. You want to tune your body instrument to support both. Kundalini yoga and meditation enable the body to free the mind from its obsession with image and turn some of its attention toward gathering knowledge and wisdom. This gathering, oddly enough, even expands the value of the image; the yoga and meditation then enable the body-mind connection to focus on this combined value.

This becomes the base for your real experience. The mind finds rest in its pre-verbal silence and relates beyond image. You make a friend of the mind rather than an enemy. This is peace of mind . . . this is a meditative mind . . . this is the new evolution of human consciousness. This is a glimpse of the future and with your discipline it can happen right now.

NOTES TO MY ANGELS:

46

A modern human lives in a marvelously calibrated worship body; it is not a work body of any sorts. We do not fly, jump, swim, lift or run as mightily as most animals. We are born, more or less, completely helpless . . . and . . . for a great reason.

Over the last seven million years of our upright two-legged evolution, nature built the human anatomy for the achievement of our ultimate human purpose . . . oneness in awareness, capable of processing enlightenment. We have reached the physical stage now, where we are crossing over from our old purpose of survival and its' many processes of physical achievement to an entirely new era. These survival emotions of fear and aggression are to now be discarded and replaced by the new evolutionary intention. It is upon us today, and for those who are paying attention, we are living it.

The human child is born helpless and innocent. The human child takes longer to mature than any other species. Even walking takes a very long time by comparison — the horse and the deer are walking within a day. Through this inborn set of frailties, we are forced to develop our higher assets of complex reasoning early on. The human child is not destined to labor, it is stimulated to awaken its' power of awareness, to expand its brilliance and enlighten itself from the collective human consciousness; being born physically helpless, aides in this journey.

Learn to observe and encourage the children as they embark on this adventure . . . it has little to do with the older, more fear-based traditions of our cultures, our religions and our national interests.

There are so many who have gone before us on this evolutionary adventure. Countless millions of generations have been used for evolving our physical bodies forward to the point of this new assignment. For eons we toiled and labored with these bodies to arrive at this place in time. We can learn from their efforts of surviving and dominating, of weaponry and war — we do not need to repeat these actions.

Our bodies are now finely tuned instruments: to be kept healthy, happy, whole and holy; to nourish with food that is food; to exercise for both strength and flexibility; and to carry our consciousness on its vast evolutionary path.

To know that our ancestors are all the time equally present in their truest sense provides a sense of gratitude for this progress. Aspects are always dying for something new to be born. One develops the next generation to be more advanced . . . not to repeat. The present child is born as a body of worship with a mind of wonder — not an action figure that wanders through insecurity and conquers with aggression. This is how these new Crystal (which means Christal in Aramaic) children are to be raised.

The early development of a modern child's [DNA] must focus on expanding consciousness or else it will become completely bored. The new human brain, built for discovery, if limited to memorization and testing — will break down. The school's focus on logic and testing will create a neurological rebellion because the creative and magical facets are being ignored. This is the root cause of dyslexia, depression and ADD/ADHD . . . epidemics in today's schools.

This same bored child grows up seeking fulfillment and relief outside itself . . . an endless battle of work without succeeding to be fulfilled, but producing a lifetime of chasing and competing with the world. When these wants are not readily met, negativity becomes a lifestyle. How many have you met today who are trapped in these skins of negativity — treated by drugs of the street, or the bar, or the pharmacy, or the workplace, or consumption?

We must transform and transpose how we raise and educate these new children. This is the next evolution. We are now crossing over the starting line in an inspired journey . . . it is time to become our greatest greatness. Love to learn to enjoy this new evolution of human consciousness . . . the greatest possibility of life is counting on you.

NOTES TO MY ANGELS:

47

Be grateful for what you have . . . be grateful for all you are. See this body as a sacred vessel carrying you from where you are to who you are. You are always connected to where you are heading, while being exactly where you are right now. This is the progression of your evolution . . . from the eternal source — to the infinite sea.

This is what we yogis call 'The River'. Your opportunity opens up when you become conscious of the river's total journey; relishing in your distant connection to this ocean (your destination) while enthusiastically embracing your moment in the journey (your now).

The cosmos (including Earth) has no vacancies - this is [its] absolute nature. When any movement (physical or mental) takes place at your location, equal movement simultaneously takes place at your destination. When you occupy the total space (The River) in this way, you are embracing not only your movement in this moment, but also the momentum of your complete vision.

You are now working with the 'Oneness' nature of creation . . . GOD . . . (the omnipresent provider) responding to the conscious openness in your request (your vision). Be very disciplined to not introduce doubt into this equation; it clouds the accuracy and disrupts the efficiency of the process.

This is the science of manifestation . . . using the power of intention — linked through the clarity of your vision — linked to persistent proper action — linked to the absolute nature of the cosmos (grace). This is what it means to become 'The River' . . . this is what it means to manifest the ocean.

NOTES TO MY ANGELS:

48

To be at peace with relationships fueled by relief — not searching for the words of comfort, but sensing the conversations of mutual purpose; this is family striking chords of conscious communication . . . bonding in their connection more deeply than ever. This is the music of the spheres; it fuels destinies to cross-pollinate and relationships to discover their mutual growth without struggle.

There are no written instructions that bring you to this place of power . . . there are instructions on the inside of consciousness that bring the discipline required to open such a place that is already with you. This discipline, known as sadhana to the ones who practice fulfillment in their life — is an action that takes place before every day takes place.

A Sadhana contains elements that cause the senses to perceive the purpose within each moment. A Sadhana contains the ingredients that permit the eyes to see the subtle clues hidden behind the obvious. A Sadhana contains the ingredients that permit the ears to hear the subtle instructions whenever new patterns appear in old relations, or brand new relations appear out of the blue. A Sadhana is a practice that puts you in touch with everything you touch. A Sadhana revitalizes your senses to experience each experience fully and knowledgeably.

Sadhana combines all of the technologies of body, mind, emotions, and spirit into a common sense working relationship. There are elements of Sadhana contained in many other practices, but when combined around a common morning purpose, they activate the most conscious and conscientious powers within you.

Take the time to learn how this can apply to your life. Take the time to touch this base within you every day. It can begin with a few minutes of mindfully breathing when you first awaken.

The starting point is a desire for happiness and fulfillment; the next step is the inspiration to follow the one before it.

NOTES TO MY ANGELS:

49

Seekers — students of the Infinite, students of yoga, students of life — often complain that when they sit down to meditate, they are not always greeted by the pleasantness of openness, the attitude of readiness, or a heartfelt sense of willingness. The great master Yogi Bhajan said many times, "If when meditating — all your garbage does not come out to greet you — you are probably not meditating."

Meditation disassembles old thought patterns and reassembles them into ones that better serve the 'pre-awakened' on the path to becoming 'awakened'. This is not always a dance — much of the time it is a struggle — especially when you run into patterns that have become attachments.

Attachments are common when patterns have been in place for many years . . . and most of every one's patterns have been. They are entrenched in the established system — the subconscious believes they are protecting your life perfectly and does not plan on giving them up that easily.

Do not be concerned; meditation is not about getting it right, it is about getting right to it and doing so daily. It is not about proving who you are . . . it is about improving who you are. It is about becoming aware of the rhythms of your life in relation to the experience of life, and getting these experiences in touch with their deeper meanings . . . in touch with your purpose.

Meditation will definitely be running into garbage here . . . if you are doing it properly. Welcome the garbage and rejoice in the joy of the exposure to the light of day . . . it will ultimately liberate you from the burden.

NOTES TO MY ANGELS:

50

Establish your passions on a day-to-day basis. Whatever you attach your conscious and undoubted passions to will manifest. This is a power and miracle of the human being actually being human . . . the light (hue) in the mind (man) has the power that no other creature does. This human worship instrument we possess as a human being allows our passion to produce — literally from out of the blue — whatever we consciously envision on Earth. No other creature has this ability — this is our advantage in a whole world of disadvantages.

There are two rather opposite directions of working consciousness into this equation of manifestation: 1) create horizons; 2) create focal points. Horizons cast and open the nets of the mind to wander, wonder and gather ideas and prospects available into the space of life. Focal points draw in this net of perception around what is present; to determine what is appropriate for any given moment of time in life. The direction of the eyes during meditation is important: when you mediate on your third eye point, you create horizons; when you meditate on the tip of your nose, you create a focal point.

Make use of meditations in this way. Establish a process of consciously envisioning; then with determined intention, remove the inappropriate doubts and develop the appropriate passions. Use the power of this human body, this human worship instrument to become the life you want to live.

NOTES TO MY ANGELS:

ASPECT SIX

The
Emotional
Body

ASPECT SIX
—The Emotional Body—

51

Over the centuries we have developed our collective human opinions around primitive emotions; an emotional body, stuffed with survival reactions that have not been advanced or revitalized for many millions of years. These opinions may hold no truth; they may only be opinions . . . but they are wrapped in ancient emotions that have no modern bearings of language to argue against them . . . so they live by default and influence us from their position in the subconscious.

Opinions want to survive, like anything does, and our emotions support this desire. Look how long the flat Earth lived in the fears of the Dark Ages.

It is now time to separate these collective opinions from their individual facts . . . even cosmic opinions need separating from their emotional support. These same cosmic opinions build and propagate our family, cultural, national, and religious stories. These are fantastic stories that fan the flames of territory, protection and intolerance, none of which were a part of the life or attitude of the family members, the national founders, or the religious Prophets. These stories are simply opinions supported by ancient collective survival emotions of humanity . . . emotions [in fact] that everyone now has to overcome.

Our opinions of this universe being a 'uni' 'verse' are the same as our older opinions of a flat Earth. It is time to upgrade our operating systems and realize just how large Infinity is.

Shame is another such opinion; a human pandemic from ancient emotions that has developed a real head of steam over the centuries. It is a 'go-to' feeling carried by many bloodlines to elicit control from others in an attempt to command safety.

The fear of death is another sensation of life that is out of tune and out of time. It is a reminder that we must not only master the instrument of life — we must keep it tuned. Without tuning, even great playing will be way off key.

When we shy from confronting to correct these erroneous opinions; we allow them to permeate and prevail. In terms of realities over opinions; we must build the collective awareness beyond these emotions if we want to spread any sense of real life. The Universe is a multi-verse; the Earth is round; life can be enlightened to see beyond the doors of death; and shame is an ancient fantasy, begging for a more conscious world to replace it. These and more are the basics to be mastered and taught.

Tune your instrument of life daily . . . be in touch, be in tune, be in time with your space always . . . this is Sadhana . . . a key to the 'new economy' in the 'next evolution'. This is growth . . . this is living life.

NOTES TO MY ANGELS:

52

A tangent of a tangent leads to an outcome that has little to do with the original intention . . . interpretations morph the original intention and allow discoveries to emerge. The lack of such exploration is the byproduct of a school system through which we are not educated, but rewarded for being right at the expense of being risky, adventurous, somewhat chaotic and even happy.

Schools of the future must teach that there has to be a degree of faith when you hit this part of your psyche . . . being inclusive of the tangent rather than demolishing it and moving on. Being able to observe the connectedness of all the impossibilities is an insight that borders on intuition. However, this is not a training of modern education and rarely explored in a society bent on results.

The arduous yet essential task leading to a tangent of a tangent is the morphing of intention to match the outcomes and then allowing outcomes to be steps to greater outcomes. This is the adventure of allowing image to transform at the heart level — the basic key to changing character through the characteristics.

There is a natural avoidance of this. It is thought (by the brain) to be only chaos. What the brain is not honoring is that in chaos there is always a connecting string; a string that might lead to an ultimate discovery. This connection does not respond, react, or even make sense to the original intention, but spontaneously erupts from the midst of nonsense. This is where the impossibilities are at their greatest possibility — if you have the discipline to remain clear and awake.

This is also a most powerful technique in which you can allow a relationship to form in the heart. Though it makes no sense to your logical mind, it is far superior to any of the logic that you have previously experienced.

This is a relationship of a magical heart . . . allow it to flourish . . . it will reward you beyond your logical imagination. This is the next evolution of human consciousness . . . this is the greatest possibility of life.

NOTES TO MY ANGELS:

53

Slow your rhythms down, efficiency is not about speed, it is about connection, traction, grip and accuracy. These all tend to fulfill a time-line faster than any speed. There is a Native American proverb: a young boy asks his Grandmother how long it will take him to accomplish his task. "Well," she answers, "it should take about a week if you set your mind to it. But if you really hurry, it will take at least two weeks."

Be un-cautious, but do not be unconscious. Small focused steps produce greater achievements because they advance and do not stumble. Small steps become the biggest steps of all, for small steps add up. Big steps can become extremely small when they fall down and stumbles require recovery.

Real-time and perceived time have a relationship. Their relationship will determine our relationship with progress. Our relationship with progress determines our relationship with hope . . . our hope determines our mood . . . our mood determines our perception, and our perception determines our sense of time.

Never allow yourself to remain uncomfortable because the present moment reminds you of the past. Never allow yourself to be uncommitted because you are unable to know how. Turn the clock forward from the past to the inspiration of now. The inspiration of now contains all the reasons of 'why'. Once you commit to these reasons of 'why', the 'how' shows up. Once you commit to this 'how' (something must be done), the inspiration arrives with a powerful commitment. This inspiration then fills to the brim with every detail required for the 'how'.

Use this in your life to have the time of your life. Use the time of your life to create the dreams of your life. Use the dreams of your life to attract relationships into your life. Share the time of your life with the relationships of your life.

This is the new evolution . . . this is the greatest efficiency and purpose of life.

NOTES TO MY ANGELS: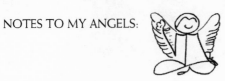

54

Fear is like an ocean — time never warms its waters while you shiver and wait. Entering slowly is not a valid strategy to make it easier either. The cold is not erased by any amount of — "waiting until you are ready".

If you are not ready now, you are not ready ever . . . that is the reality of time's illusion . . . "what is to be, already is" (Humee Hum Brahm Hum). Until you make your readiness active, your readiness is sleeping.

Being ready is an action to act upon — not a condition to wait for. Ready is the courageous act of facing fears that are always present in everyone. Ready is the courageous act of facing these fears until they no longer face you — control you — limit you. Ready is about connecting with your projection . . . not your protection.

We tend to self-talk and guide life with words learned and crafted as an infant. They make up the weakest parts of our current story . . . with very little glory. These are the genetic fears of illusion's preservation — long past their actual usefulness — transferred through the generations in this day. Commitment is the antidote to these deep genetic stories. Breaking the codes of this family language overrides the way your world is controlled from deep within history. This allows you to be courageously present in the present moment.

Courage is entering time to maximize it, not running ahead of it, or lagging behind it. When you run ahead of time, you are anxious and jittery in the present — when lagging behind, it becomes exhaustive and trepidation clouds even the simplest tasks. Pay the greatest attention to your positive, committed emotions at this moment; they will guide you forward and introduce you to 'how'. Be disciplined to experience — but do not act upon — all the negative voices that will naturally arise to produce the equal opposition.

Is this a huge challenge? Absolutely — yes it is — but dive in and deal with the cold waters. It will never get any warmer, but the swim will always turn out to be fabulous.

NOTES TO MY ANGELS: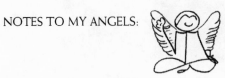

55

When you have perfected the dance with your patterns and your performance of your habits has become quite seamless — change is difficult. Any change to your habits must enter through a crack of perceived imperfection . . . a seam in the pattern of your perfected dance. Herein lies the dilemma . . . there appears to be no seams and your perfection will defend this appearance.

All the information that is required to change is always present within you; this is the nature of the Cosmos. However, this information presents itself as eccentric, as chaotic, as random and confused and when highly pressurized, it represents anxiety. None of these options are attractive to a perfected dance.

Remember: this perfected dance is marketable for your survival, but not your happiness.

When you desire change — in order to receive this new information — you must perform your old perfected dances with a flaw. Such a flaw will bring discomfort and embarrassment. Pass into the pain of this embarrassment willingly, and enthusiastically as the flaws in your performance stumble forward through new patterns. These new patterns will allow the changes to emerge through their seams and cracks.

Yoga, meditation, singing, chanting, Chi Gung, Tai Chi, Pran Krya and many more, are all methods of defining and aligning the body with the psyche. When such information is defined and aligned, it stops producing clouds and fogginess and allows for greater clarity. This is one of the human goals of consciousness known as super-intuition. Trusting the imperfections in these moments is a surrendering of your control to the cosmic perfection. This is extremely powerful . . . every human has every right to this power, but this power is surrounded by your resistance to surrendering. To give your 'self' the authority to use this right is a fundamental step toward fulfillment of life's purpose. There is never any need to know how to perform this process. Fill your attitude with a massive declaration of 'why' — the 'how' will appear.

In other words, "When is now a good time?"

NOTES TO MY ANGELS:

56

Anxiety and panic are not bad, they are actually a good thing . . . they are just too much of a good thing. Anxiety and panic are the by-product of a disorganized and non-indexed akashic record — the human super-memory.

The akashic records holds on to all memory of every experience that has ever happened ever. Along with the memory of the event, information, wisdom and knowledge gained from the event is also stored here. This is why it is known as a super-memory. This is a massive database completely linked to your existence containing the multi-incarnation recordings of everything that has happened in every existence up to this moment.

When the akashic records are disorganized, chaotic . . . not indexed . . . and the urgent need arises for the information — the entire database is compassionately dumped into your body through the solar plexus. Knowledge and wisdom arrive on the coattails of an intense moment, but it is scrambled and the result is anxiety. The system knows that the information you so desperately require is in there somewhere so it gives you the entire load. It is up to you to sort it out,

Pouring through the solar plexus, the root of the akasha, a gut wrenching sensation takes place in the body. The rush of information twists and torques from the belly up to the throat, pulling it all into a gigantic body knot. This is panic and anxiety. This is why we say it is a good thing . . . just too much of a good thing.

At the core of this there is a cure . . . it requires effort . . . spend time every day organizing and indexing the akasha. Accomplish this through conscious breathing and conscious moving. Use yoga, Chi Gung and Tai Chi, chanting mantras and vipassana (meditation on silence). Do this on a daily basis and eventually, when the need arrives, your system will access the information required without having to sort through such a vast database to find the few necessities. You ultimately learn to solve and resolve your exact challenges, discomforts and dilemmas with grace. This trades panic and anxiety attacks for moments of super-intuitive insight. The exact information required is delivered to you — not dumped on you. This is the way of the new evolution — the way of grace and joy.

NOTES TO MY ANGELS:

57

What if the next time you have an emotionally painful experience, you do not run away from it? What if, by not avoiding this event, you actually have the experience of the experience of the event? What if, by consciously breathing during this experience of the event, you calm yourself?

What if, within this calm, you reduce all reference to "other" . . . another cause as the cause; the sensation as something other than you; another time without this sensation; another person as the cause of this sensation . . . what if? What would it be like if this externalizing was not the dominant pattern in your psyche?

This would be the outskirts of the suburbs of the village of your liberation. This would be the gateway to your freedom. This would be the path to the castle of your prosperity and fulfillment and all the pain and reference to other is the moat of your pain surrounding it.

Dive into the moat . . . swim through your pain . . . cross over it and reach your castle. This castle contains your purpose, your fulfillment and all that you have been living for. It has always been here with you . . . waiting for you to awaken.

Welcome to the new evolution. You are one of the early pioneers.

NOTES TO MY ANGELS:

58

To center yourself in pressured, stressful or chaotic environments — to locate and shed any dissociation that these cause — then fully experience your intended experience; this is living . . . actually living.

Sit and focus on the simple act of your breathing. Focus first on breathing from your diaphragm. Once you have fully connected to the diaphragm sensation, add the tip of your nose to your conscious awareness. Locate your sense of self in the experience of this breathing . . . the diaphragm drawing breath through the tip of your nose and into the lungs. Do this for at least three minutes every day. This is the minimum contribution to connecting spirit.

Breathing is an essential component of living . . . by focusing your awareness on it, you ground your body with your brain and then with your environment. This is the simplest of the 'mindfulness meditation' forms. It may seem simple, but it is very potent. Mindfulness increases the brain's connection to each present moment by causing the production of electrochemical charges. These connect the sensory system, to the nervous system, to the glands and organs, back to the nervous system and onto the brain—producing sensations, thoughts, calculations, and then attitudes of calm.

By comparison, life under stress is a jumble of chaotic stimulations leading to reactive thoughts. When we are not mindful, the brain delivers these random options as noise. This noise constructs insistent, convincing brain waves that give no relief, that give no calm or peace, but become our interpretations of reality.

Learn to make this meditation a primary response to pressure and stress. Learn to become masterful in the spiritual realm and your physical world. This is the power that is required going forward . . . mastery of all realms. Our planet needs this; our planet needs you.

NOTES TO MY ANGELS:

59

This planet is an 'enclosed' system . . . it will run out of natural resources if we do not practice renewal. We, as humans, are also an enclosed system . . . we will run out of human resources if we do not practice renewal. Learn to associate with a healthy intolerance of the ignorant habits that ignore this reality. This is an intolerance that you should welcome . . . then you become your authority; you become your living asset.

Work with these stages of emotional evolution. Nearly everyone has graduated from their early infant stage of (envy with frustration). Most of the planet has also incorporated the young child's capacity of (jealousy with anger). Some more are able to conjure up the pre-pubescent response of (observation with determination). But there are so very few who have achieved their pubescent evolutionary stage of imagination combined with a curious quest. Almost no one in this world has become an adult — a true adult — using inspired purpose with absolute commitment.

These are the five stages of Human Emotional Evolution. When missing — they plague our lives . . . when present — they guide us. Being educated in these and stable in their social contribution will become a shared necessity within the new evolution.

Be a pioneer — first one on your block — become a leader who re-educates yourself. Take yourself from puberty, or whatever level you were detained at, then move along to true adulthood. You will find yourself a practitioner of real meaning — congratulations — you have become a mentor to the masses. They need it though they may object . . . it will not be easy, but it will eventually be rewarding.

NOTES TO MY ANGELS:

60

To stop an argument — first stop arguing — then speak with the fragrance of resolution, not the stink of confrontation. The louder the opposition wants to yell . . . the softer and more confidently you want to speak. Be an example of a pure existence having a pure experience.

Arguments stem from doubt . . . using the anger to force verification of a value that you yourself do not fully believe. Convincing another through an argument is actually striving to convince you.

It is more effective to work the inside. Achieve inner approval and no longer require it from the outside . . . no longer require others to validate you . . . no argument needed. Employ your life-force as a means of being . . . . all that you are becomes merely what you are . . . all that you are engaged in becomes engaged.

Experience your existence and remove the arguments that deny it — nothing to justify . . . or verify. Experiencing this without the need for a witness to validate your experience — when no witness is required, no argument is required.

This is a state of grace . . . this is true compassion . . . this is peace of mind and fulfillment of the heart. This is you, loving and leading by example.

NOTES TO MY ANGELS:

61

Tension, pressure, stress and friction are the human consciousness impressed by gravity. Without gravity and these four impressions, there is no possibility of life, or any other 'matter' in this universe.

How you interpret the message from these impressions of gravity will determine how you feel about the world around you. At any given moment, how do you view your possibilities of moving forward? These views will cause all of your decisions. Am I supported in my dreams? Is the world out to get me and destroy my dreams or is it friendly? These questions will cause responses . . . I will succeed! . . . or . . . I will have problems!

All of these and many other questions with responses will arise on a daily basis and shape the ways you view the essential impressions of gravity. Since these impressions are a natural part of all existence, it is really up to you to make them work.

Mold your opinions and responses to all the tension, pressure, stress and friction existing everywhere around you. Cause your responses to promote and project the greatness of your existence. Work to align all your bodies (physical as well as emotional and mental) in such a way that your relationships with their impressions of gravity are productive tools creating the world you want to live in.

React to the essential realities of tension, pressure, stress and friction with real, supportive and promoting decisions. In this way you progress.

NOTES TO MY ANGELS:

62

Pleasure is found in whom we know — what we do — where we are . . . happiness exists with wherever, whenever and whoever we are. Happiness is wired into human DNA . . . pleasure gets us all wired up in the chase to locate it on the outside. Happiness is our birthright . . . pleasure is found in the hierarchies of our birthing.

The most important conclusion to draw — as early in life as possible — is the conclusion that allows you to set your own course. This will become where your greatest challenges dwell. You must face the worst fears in this process . . . they will try to force you to give up and run back. It is your job to dive deeper into the core of your being and move forward.

When you move forward, you also bump into the seeds of happiness along the way. Plant them in the soil of your dreams and nourish them with each and every day.

And by the way — those fears that you found surrounding the core of your being when you set this course; they will not go away . . . you will have to re-employ them on some other task if you do not want to be hounded by their persistence.

NOTES TO MY ANGELS:

63

Magic happens when we stop using fear and doubt to interfere with the infinite capacity of the Cosmos. Magic is the way of the feminine (the Ma). Logic is the way of the masculine (the Law).

Today's world does not readily acknowledge the power of MA (which appears to the untrained senses as chaos). The world is consumed by its obsession with LAW . . . and the predictability of ORDER. This is the world of a child needing the predictability of order to feel safe. This is the world that produces GOD as a disciplinarian — a father figure — the world of the exclusive logic.

This attitude will soon be forced from the grip of humanity as the era changes. This is what we are beginning to experience at this time as the logical pressures mount. The more you are open to magic, the more you will feel centered and at peace in these changing times.

The new evolution is one that engages GOD as the balance of both male and female. It is where awareness opens to the infinite possibility of reality rather than the limited predictability of a particular law.

NOTES TO MY ANGELS:

64

Happiness does not come from thought. Happiness happens when whatever thoughts that there are — are assembled clearly, transparently and simply. Even amongst complexities, there is always a point of simple clarity. Search for this point by knowing it exists. This knowing becomes a kind of guarantee; it uses a neurological absolute as an advantage point. What is to be already is —accurately perceives what is and appreciates what can be into existence. Happiness employs this pattern — this neurological framework — to receive the next moment from the ripples of joy. Appreciation leads to clarity, leads to moments of simplicity, leads back to happiness . . . as the song goes: "happiness runs in a circular motion . . . . . ."

Because success is the result of many failures; there are no pre-conditions, no suppositions, no previous requirements for the success of happiness. It can arise from any moment at any moment. From each failure (and its sadness) it is up to you to assemble a new moment — a next moment filled with appreciation, clarity, transparency and simplicity. Within the new assembled construct after each failure, it is additionally up to you to perceive what can become and appreciate it into existence. From this undistorted point of appreciation you anticipate the next moment respectively and receptively.

This is not something that can be thought about to be brought about; this is something that can only be 'entrained' through consistent discipline. In the same way you would discipline a tennis swing to create topspin, a golf swing to create intended direction, a violin fingering to have the harmonic spacing, a sentence to impart understanding . . . all by attempting, practicing and mirroring an imagination of it working.

Happiness is not desired or acquired; happiness is allowed to arise. Happiness is never stiff; it is as flexible as water. If at first it does not succeed . . . it will try and try and try again until it does. Such is the resilient nature of happiness.

NOTES TO MY ANGELS:

65

Time and space reward excellence — or we should more accurately state that — timespace rewards excellence, for they are a single event. This excellence, however, is only achieved through many trials all containing many mistakes and many errors. To keep-up — to maintain integrity — throughout these trials, to overcome the disappointments from the constant errors and mistakes is uniquely a human ability — a human quality. No other animal is graced with this capacity and yet humans constantly resist its application because of pride and feelings.

Such a quality (keeping up and moving forward in the midst of constant errors) is often accompanied by low self-esteem and low self-love . . . for good reason. This path — where the self view contends with the insults of many errors — would never be possible in the midst of great pride. So therefore the system protects itself and attempts to improve itself through a lowered sense of self that will not be offended by the natural folly. This low self-esteem stimulates the self to improve itself in a blinded and foolish kind of way. This stimulates self growth while shielding the painful comedy of errors from the stage of many errors.

There comes a time in every job however, when even the best tool must be released and the task of the tool declared done. If after the nail has been driven in, you still swing the hammer, you will damage the job that has been achieved. This is the case with low self-love and self-esteem. When these creativity drivers have completed their goal, you can proceed no further with them in place. They must be released. This is never easy; their process has become reliant and grown familiar — a habit pattern has formed and must now be broken.

The way to break this pattern is by honoring the work that they (the low self-esteem and low self-love) have already achieved. This is the tricky part ... honoring their work and re-assigning them to yet another level of your development.

Perhaps you can assign them to keeping you humble. You will require humbleness as your excellence continues to grow. What a great new assignment! These old tools (the low self-esteem and low self-love) will love you for it and not get in your way with it . . . which they would if you were not showing this appreciation. It is not as if they are independent beings that you must deal with. They are living parts of your being and this is an energy dance of extremely high awareness. It is both an art and a science.

The lesson is to find all the great reasons within the essence of every challenge — then honor these reasons for being what they are. In a material universe, where every action has an equal and opposite reaction, learn to redirect the angle of the reaction so that it continues working in favor of the action.

NOTES TO MY ANGELS:

ASPECT SEVEN

Communication
and
Relationships

ASPECT SEVEN
— Communication & Relationships —

66

The human voice sits between the heart and the head. When we consciously mature and grow up in spirit; we learn to use this voice to activate our heart's sense of the 'eternal' as a means of overcoming the head's addiction to temporal logic. Eternity is not at all logical.

With this activated sensation, we are able to dispose of the fear of time, the fear of its passage and the fear of our aging. If we do not dispose of this fear, we are constantly concerned with the passage of time . . . aging becomes the enemy rather than the messenger of wisdom.

All enlightened cultures are in awe of aging . . . it is worshipped as becoming closer to the goal of life. To them it is the great liberator from the darkness of ignorance. Western/industrial cultures tend to fear aging and are in awe of youth — as such — all things immature and senseless are marketed and promoted endlessly. This is one of the many reasons we pollute and destroy our planet so willingly. As immature beings, we take little responsibility for the consequences of our actions . . . just as small children are not capable of understanding the adult's reaction to their actions.

2010 and the subsequent years are the perfect times to change our communication patterns. It is a time for us to use our voice and tune this human instrument to the harmony of the heart's courage along with the head's knowledge. This is the state of consciousness from which profound wisdom arises. Our voice — resting on the heart and responding to the brain — brings great clarity when properly and powerfully balanced.

Perfect exercises to strengthen this relationship are singing in the morning to call upon your most enthusiastic (in Theo - in GOD) personality. Let yourself know each day that you speak from your own perspective and you do so with authority.

Each morning is an opportunity to be the person you were born to be. Each morning is an opportunity to take this chance . . . take this risk . . . blossom into the new evolution of human consciousness . . .create the greatest possibility of your life.

The lesson is to find all the great reasons within the essence of every challenge — then honor these reasons for being what they are. In a material universe — where every action has an equal and opposite reaction — learn to redirect the angles of the reaction to favor the action. Such is the resilient nature of the new evolution . . . such is the life that is alive today.

NOTES TO MY ANGELS:

67

When it comes to educating children in this world, one size does not fit all. Within the categories we have already labeled — the so-called unable, the disabled, the special needs and those lacking particularly common abilities — rests other advanced abilities excitedly sprinkled amongst these children with unusual and phenomenal capacities. Children are, in fact, able to see this world through a wide variety of lenses if we allow them to.

Our job as educators is not to label and categorize the child's abilities, but to excite our own ability of enabling their dormant powers . . . unique powers resting within every child on Earth. Our task is to invoke the discovery process, not define it.

Discovery is an adventure of common sense in the makes no sense in the world of 'growing up' . . . it is professionally known as education. True education, however, is a two-way road where you learn and receive as much as you teach and give.

The joys in such an educational system lie within the purposeful discovery of your 'unique' intelligence. Joy becomes a purpose, and joyful education then produces clear understandings where mis-understandings previously dominated.

Wars between cultures are most often waged when misunderstandings are unable to be intelligently resolved. When we cease to under fund education, and when we place as much research into its industry as we currently do for the military industry; we will create a world that requires little in the way of such weaponry. Then the human profits will soar on the wings of the human prophets. Intelligence, resulting from progressive — highly researched — discovery oriented education, will find common ground through commonsense, and a common wealth for the common good.

This is one of many paths toward world peace . . . a far less destructive and disheartening way than fighting for it.

NOTES TO MY ANGELS:

68

Living - true - relationships: these are connections with observations for participation . . . never . . . inspections with judgment for performance.

When you experience the fulfillment of such a relationship — a living - true - relationship — you have an awareness of connection without any credits for the performance. It is effortless . . . it is painless . . . it is gratifying.

There are many options in every moment of life, but in such a true relationship you are without options. You have surrendered all of your options to your commitment . . . and this is why — even though they are desired – living – true - relationships are generally avoided.

You fear giving up your options (they represent safety nets and backup plans) and these kind of authentic relationships are where options are no longer options. Survival instincts tell you to run like the wind.

Touch the teachings of the greatest masters - "be as death while alive," they tell you, "have no options." When you have this as a choice of no choice, you are at the gates of surrender at all times. This is authenticity; sit and seek no results in it . . . just be in this state of complete zero — shunya. This is the gateway to the land of miracles. You cannot calculate your way into this land, but once you are in — you do not want to leave — you have the time of your life — you become a beacon for others.

Survival is the instinctual avoidance of death. Death is only a death of the five senses and the five elements . . . not of the being. Grief and mourning at a death are the gauges that sit on the dash board of life; they indicate the fragility of awareness, not of life. These emotions are not bad; though they are painful, they are powerful indicators of the inner movements in awareness that is now required. This is the movement needed to relocate the eternal threads and infinite facets of the relational connections. These are what are known as the ecto-plasmic connections.

This is all about the power of subtle moments — this is a moment requiring deep and uninterrupted meditation. Do not avoid or ignore this sadness — use it to shift the physical gears over to their non-physical natures. When sadness indicates you are off this course — pause, recalibrate, and recommit to reconciling it. Do not change the sadness — change the course. Pass through sadness and exchange the ecto-plasmic connections for the connections of pure spirit that exist just "beyond" the physical.

In living - true – relationships — with choices that are no longer of your choosing and where there are no options in the options — you have completely let go of holding back. You have no plan "B" and there is no back-doors available. There is only the most valuable possession possible . . . the relationships beyond the doorway of death. The five elements and the five senses have been left at this doorway; the physical limitations are now transcended, but the relationship is even more alive and far truer.

This passage is arduous, but worth the pain. All living - true - relationships are a dress rehearsal for this death. This is why they are so obviously and adamantly avoided . . . simply remind yourself — death cannot be.

When you willingly release your intense fears of surrender and arrive at the eternity of living - true – relationship — from such a moment onward you will find yourself in fear of nothing. You will find yourself in the sweet embrace of fearless wisdom. You will find yourself . . . .

NOTES TO MY ANGELS:

69

The current evolution — the one that has been going on for billions of years — has been developing the ability of sensory perception for the purpose of protection in order to survive long enough to grow, develop and prosper. All of the senses are keyed to protecting and advancing the individual physically, but this has had very little to do with developing the capacity for emotional fulfillment.

Protection requires the ability to perceive with distinction, to create clear observation to comprehend the separations . . . we are very accurate at this. Now this is all changing; separation no longer provides protection, separation in a crowded world is creating dissociation and has become dangerous by creating mistrust. Our philosophies around the world are dynamically separated; our religions are producing fanatic positioning where we do not consider ourselves to be friends with all these observed differences. Then, when our languages are separated, we are unable to understand the subtleties of each other's attitudes and the meaning of each other's lives.

To not see each other as a friend when our population grows from 6.5 to 7 to 8 to 10 billion people will not be workable . . . a trigger point of stress will snap the system. Perception for protection had been a focal point for evolution thus far — it is the nature of nature — but this is now to shift. The frequency of the Cosmos in the new evolution is shifting and driving life in an entirely new direction. The new evolution's reason for perception will be connection. It has to be and will fail in any other way. This is extremely uncomfortable to the non-suspecting; for millions of years protection has made us safe. Now this is no longer the case and cannot be the case; from today onward if we are not connected — heart to heart — no one is going to be safe.

The next evolution can be boiled down to a very simple statement: it is the shifting of perception from safety to connectivity. What is the old saying? Keep your friends close, keep your enemies closer. Connection is the new protection. Mutual wellbeing is the new survival. If you keep your enemies close for a long enough period of time, they cease being your enemy. When we become mutually familiar, we become mutually understanding — and mutual understanding is a lasting relationship.

We have to recalibrate our senses — our sensory system — in order to achieve this. We have to recalibrate that which controls our consciousness unconsciously.

Because, even though we have an intellectual understanding . . . to a degree we have an emotional sense of connection . . . we are slightly associated with strangers around us . . . we are still instinctively driven by millions of years of protection programming running in the background of our brains. We choose to feel unsafe as a means of safety . . . it is programmed into the collective unconscious.

There are two aspects to the unconscious: these are the subconscious and the super-conscious. The subconscious drives the emotions; and the super-conscious, drives the devotions. The subconscious tries to establish our protection and the super-conscious tries to establish our connection. Both our emotions and our devotions will require significant recalibration. We have built in protection policies in each of them.

We have considered the emotions already, but what of the devotions? We have previously designed our heroic figures and religious icons based around their mightiness. Mightiness in the realms of insecurity; strength with a sword in the midst of life's battles; the entire concept of God the Father; all of this is going to require transformation.

God has been the Father figure for thousands of years because a father is the protector and provider. In the new phase of evolution, God will not have a single gender . . . definitely not as a "father-figure" . . . because, in reality, there is no reproduction if God is just a father — no father gives birth. The next evolution is about being real and connected and aware of realities.

This is a major shift — cultures are going to be redesigned and redefined by the very nature of the times. People are going to rebel from this and we can see it in the fanatic nature of religions today. Our philosophies, all of our civilities, everything down to the core will be changing. How does that make you feel? Those who want to preserve the way things have always been are going to become frantic with this. Feeling very unsafe will become the common experience as we move forward and it will depend on our compassion as to how we treat each other in the process. Because unconsciously the collective human mind is deeply attached to the ways that have been . . . thought processes, of thousands of years, will all be shifting.

Become a leader in the procession. Become a pioneer in your area. But do not push it; just let the wave of compassionate timespace carry us all forward. When we push, there will be push back. Become the new evolution with grace and the possibilities of life beyond war, beyond violence and beyond protection.

NOTES TO MY ANGELS:

70

Everything in life is a relationship. In our primary relationships — the ones near the epicenter of our activity — it is never productive to wait for relating to happen. You must creatively create each moment in order for momentum to take place. Guarantee the consistency of each outcome consistently. When outcomes appear to be blocked, remember; all any blockage represents is a perfect opportunity to begin. "No," is a starting point.

Use every blockage like a workout gym. Understand that the heavier the relational weight, the greater the relational possibility. Often times these relational weights are from ancient karmic memories that have grown into present moment "monsters" through many lifetimes of neglect. Also, relationships that are extremely enjoyable but lack the sparkling chemistry; these are huge gifts from the ancient past as well. Sparkle is but an illusion — an illusion that can be built and then enjoyed if you learn to do the work.

A physical/chemical attraction (great chemistry) is the simple comparison of angles, genetic patterns at the core structure of your DNA. In this core of all DNA are crystals that refract and reflect the light that carries all information and the patterns of this are what creates all the sensations we refer to as chemistry. If this is the main driving force, the main attraction in a relationship; it will all be highly stimulating, but definitely shallow. And by modern court records — predictably temporal — divorce rates are very high today and this is one of the main contributions to this fact. Sparkle is the goal and sparkle is fleeting.

This is why more conscious traditional cultures relied on arranged relationships. Here, a far more permanent event was gathered around . . . the compatibility of core-consciousness. To be with a best friend who — rather than measuring what they were getting out of you — had your gift of many lifetimes in their blood; this was the deepest and most meaningful of all relational experiences. Entering into these vast fields of like-mindedness; discovering lifetimes spent with such a partnership; the fascination and passion surfaces years later amongst the depths of trust.

The pathway of enlightenment is of course the fundamental purpose of all existence. Is this your destiny in this life? This is an advanced course and not of much interest to the elementary mind. Are you more enchanted by your chemistry of a moment, or your ministry to the cosmos?

Contrary to the films of Hollywood and Bollywood; there is rarely a relationship that is off the shelf, out of the box, and ready to be used without a great deal of assembly. This assembly process can take many years to accomplish . . . that is, if one really applies sufficient concentration and works without the common setbacks of despair. Are you ready for this work? When one side goes to frailty — are you ready to go to your strength . . . when one side goes to confusion or bewilderment — are you ready to not go to protection and condemnation.

When any partnership is fragile, faith must compassionately prevail as the mender of hearts. This is not an arena for anyone who dislikes consequences, for the consequences in a relationship are often instantaneous and momentous. After all, relationships are mirrors of the spirit.

Relationships are great teachers. They teach that life is not about changing or controlling the outside world — life is about molding and mastering the perceptions from the inside. Never demand, always compassionately command any union. Commanding is the 'co' (togetherness) of the 'mand' (minds). Thoughts formed from these tethered together minds display the possibilities of life and break the illusions that bind us short of our dreams. Learn to limit the thoughts that do not serve or further life's possibilities . . . or that produce ill will. Learn to have the authority that achieves mental and emotional clarity. Remember: you are the one who thinks and feels your thoughts and feelings. Make the choices that allow you to relate, not the ones that refuse or confuse or self-protect by remaining closed.

Relational success is never found with competition or comparison. As long as there is comparing going on, there is not relating. Be compassionate and compatible for others to aspire; be compassionate and compatible and you are one whom others will admire; be compassionate and compatible and you will recognize the other person as yourself. Then remember: every event in life — even being by your-self — is a relationship. Strive to be the best participant possible.

NOTES TO MY ANGELS:

71

The planet Mercury has significant influence on our communication. Communication creates the quality and caliber of our relationships. Relationships require pace and being on pace requires practice . . . it is never set by itself. There must be a conscious effort to arrive at the pace of life for any relationship existing within the space you are living . . . so that the outer world and the inner world are harmonious . . . are in unison. Learn to obtain the harmonic intervals that work for working together.

The wave of time (space moving through the position of now) will not carry you on to your goal when you hold back or push faster than it rolls. Angles, timing, balance, synchronizing, being sensitive to your total environment and being flexible enough to respond, all require tremendous effort and a great deal of insistent — persistent — consistent practice.

When this kind of pace is established it is known as a parallel relationship. You are pacing your environment; you are pacing your life and you pacing the lives of those around you. With all of this parallel pacing — harmonious movement forward becomes effortless.

There is a very practical effort, a pragmatic investment that delivers this seemingly miraculous return. It is logical input with a magical outcome, the human being — being humane. This is the new evolution and it honors your highest purpose.

NOTES TO MY ANGELS:

72

For generations, centuries and millennia, we the people of this world have shared our stories of the world — that world "out there" — the external one that appears to be other than the self. We see this as our experiences and our relationships and we all agree that it is there . . . this world "out there."

We have constructed great entertaining adventures to describe this world and prejudices to differentiate ourselves from it . . . all revolving around the assumption that there is a self — and then there is a world (out there) that is other than the self. For this particular inspirational lesson – let us refer to that external-world as the "grand-other" . . . that which appears to be other than self.

What if you were to discover that the "grand-other" is not actually out there — it is not actually other than you and we have all simply lost the capacity to see our oneness, our unity . . . the absolute connection. What if we were to discover that a greater part of life's purpose, the most important part of our conscious growth pattern, was to break this illusion . . . this inability to see the total connection of all things? What if we were to do something to create a routine — a routine that engaged in a sort of detective search for the answer — the "PIN" number one might say? What if we explored the universe for this code that accesses the ability to disassemble the perception of the "grand-other" as being other than the self?

Would this be empowering? If you corrected this collective mental concept and regained your ability to see beyond this illusion — would this solve many challenges, answer many questions?

A truly conscious person does this instead of attempting to change the "grand other." A truly conscious person understands the illusion — every one and every thing is refraction, is reflection, a magnification of a facet of the self. A truly conscious person does not have the prejudice of seeing the other as other.

The Buddha said it best, "When you see worthiness, praise it . . . When you see unworthiness, look for the common thread connecting to you." The truly conscious person accepts the wholeness of all matter and applies this perception without preference to life and all its events . . . seeing the "grand-other" as a lesson full of messages.

Family and loved ones and close associates; in addition to the greatest love, will present us with the parts of ourselves that we have stumbled over, ignored and avoided for lifetimes. This is a great part of family's responsibility and can make them — at times — the most irritating of all associations, the most challenging of all relationships, but also the most important ones to learn from.

It is as if everyone in your "grand-other" is a blank screen. We are projecting onto them — then receiving images back. Some events, instead of being a blank screen are like a black hole . . . no matter how much light you shine, it's absorbed and disappears. These are the most challenging of all relations . . . these are the hardest lessons to learn.

Create a meditative and contemplative routine on a daily, weekly, monthly basis — one that establishes consistently, emotionally and psychologically — a view of the "grand-other" as being you, a facet of you. This is the true relationship . . . this is a human being — being humane. It honors your highest self.

NOTES TO MY ANGELS:

73

Mercury is the planet that rules our communication — communication rules our relationships — everything in life is a relationship. Therefore, Mercury has a hand in everything.

The Mercury finger (the pinky) is formed when you are an embryonic ball in the womb — it is formed from the exact same tissue as the frontal lobe of the brain. This are of the brain contains a complex network of nerve endings and neurons for higher reasoning . . . home of the highest frequencies in the human psyche. Here, your perceptions of the self communicate back to the self . . . out from this sense of self, all relationships are formed.

This is known as the mirroring facility of relationship . . . the observer and the observed. Can you keep up with the vitality of these events that promote the relating in a relation? Or — if no connection appears — do you blame this lack of connection on the mirror? This blame is always far — far from truth. However, when it worms its way into your thinking and appears in your world, it becomes your truth, which is not truth, but . . . the illusion of this confusion is pandemic.

In reality, the observed and the observer are the same event. The only question is how long will it take humanity to commit to the reality of this universal principle? When will our eyes see and our senses connect to the oneness of everything? When will we decide to honor our right to have the rite of a relation-ship — rather than a capsizing relation-canoe? When will we decide to stand up in our unions and experience the powers of relation with fulfillment and joy? Remember: you can always stand up in a ship, but do not try it in a canoe.

When will we stop the illusion of blaming the mirror for the image it reflects . . . for how we feel what we feel . . . for how we are experiencing our experience? The image in the mirror is not different and never separate from the object standing before it. We are the objects before the mirror of our experience. The observed and the observer are, in fact, one and we are always equal to our predicament. The motive and the motivation are — in fact — the same. If you are not experiencing yourself everywhere, where are you and what is it that you are experiencing? Where then can you possibly experience you if not everywhere? Believing you experience your self in some places and moments and not in others is the pure cruelty of duality.

The only question possible when you desire a true relationship is . . . When is now a good time? . . . not . . . When will the right relationship show up? Ready, is a verb that acts through the actions of self-realization and then promotes the rite of a relationship to show up . . . not the right relationship.

Ask yourself — what is being placed before me — how do I experience myself in it? If you lack the attention to do this, you will only experience the tension . . . never the lesson. This is then not the mastery of life at all; it is the mystery of hell. To walk out of this hell is the journey of your struggle — the krya in your mirror.

To master this is a very advanced course of life — is it not? Are you "ready" for such a level of difficulty? If your desire is yes, then buckle up and get along with it. Creation will produce a miracle of illusions — but then, what else would you expect from an Infinite Source.

Accept the other as yourself and welcome it home to your Heaven on Earth. This introduces your mirroring facility of relationship; where, when you honor the other, you honor your highest self.

NOTES TO MY ANGELS:

74

The human being is a social animal. When you befriend those in your life, you must accept them with all their quirks and all their qualities. Any relationship must be viewed through the eyes of gravity, the eyes of levity, and the eyes of neutrality combined. These are the three aspects of the collective human consciousness and each is required for a relationship to have any chance in this material world.

Without the discipline and the support of levity to guide you through this maze, entropy will bring in gravity and any relationship will fall down. It is the law . . . things fall apart . . . gravity wins when left as the sole ruler through its fear. Gravity pulls everything down; do not take this personally, just take it to heart — it is a law that cannot be avoided. Respond to gravity with levity rather than with unrestrained emotions.

This emotional body is set up and managed by the glands and organs of your physical body. This emotional body is the key to levity. The glands and organs are affected by the food we eat, the postures we stand and sit with, our physical activities, our prior habits and to a great part — our DNA. In order to alter your emotions you must address each of these elements, from your diet to your emotional DNA.

All emotional DNA has every aspect; their influence on our attitudes is caused by whatever parts of this DNA that are activated. With deep meditative work, this formula can be changed. Activate the appropriate pieces and the genetic patterns are shaped and sculpted accordingly.

Remember: relationships are just that — boats co-occupied in which you cooperate and collaborate to coexist as sailors through the winds of timespace. Working on any relationship begins with accessing your personal participation and leveraging the most out of all your greatest qualities.

Prepare your contribution to the relation with each breath . . . deliver this sensation of truly living . . . foster the sensation that you were sent to Earth to experience and build upon the connections in life. This will cause you to experience your life as it is and as it can be.

NOTES TO MY ANGELS:

75

While building the tribes into community, while building a relationship into unity; you will either establish identity through your excellence or your obstinance. By being collaborative, not competitive, you are envisioning an ideal content, while disposing consciously of its impenetrable packaging. You are allowing the balance to balance the polarities . . . both the positives and the negatives.

In the process, display great patience . . . patience is not sitting and waiting, it's sitting and knowing. Patience is holding the 'space' of achievement with the 'place' of absolute willingness. In the sailing of a relationship . . . (Place) is the position of your sails. (Destiny) is where you are going. (Purpose) is the pathway between where you are and where you are going. The winds are the circumstances of the infinite possibilities of the (Space). In these infinite possibilities are the infinite solutions awaiting your patience to unfold them.

In the process of building this community — social, business or other — trust everyone for who they are and allow them to be who they are . . . all the while having tremendous encouragement for them becoming who they long to be. Remember: all life — at the core — longs to be included . . . never excluded — longs to be inclusive . . . not exclusive.

To this end; it is essential that your voice be reasonable in tone, while you are unreasonable in your commitment. There can be no audible absolutes on your voice-print of this commitment — the tone must be flexible and yet the commitment absolutely firm. Absolutes in your tone will always set up a rebuttal, which will in turn set up an argument. When your tone is flexible and there is a guarantee in your absolute commitment, there is nothing to rebut and you convey a sense of total security.

Patience, when accompanied by such security, is a guarantee . . . your needs will be met by the gratitude that your needs will be met. Humee hum . . . Brahm hum . . . this is Sanskrit for such a realization.

NOTES TO MY ANGELS: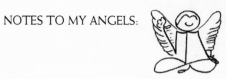

76

When you believe that anything outside yourself will change the quality of your life, you are like the kitten seeing its reflection in a mirror and thinking there are two cats in the room. It is the quality of your commitment to the self that determines the quality of your life as well as the quality of your relationships to others. The quality of these relationships creates the quality of your experience.

In this relation to the self, be ever aware of both your strengths and your weaknesses . . . your assets and your debt . . . and be committed to both. Do not be depressed by your debts — your weakness — simply understand that you love them, or else you would not have them. You require them to learn the lessons of their perspective and without them you would not be complete in this moment.

The only way to fully enjoy your great wealth — your many strengths and assets — is to be able to withstand the pressure of this debt. The only way to truly appreciate the experience of your existence is to see strength and weakness, asset and debt, as a carefully balanced balance sheet . . . a full picture of you. Be able to look at your debts and instantly balance this view with your assets . . . the shadow gives perspective to the light in any "real" picture. This follows the old proverb of successful living, "When you are depressed . . . press back."

When you see your world in this way, the world will rush to you as a great and stable investment. People will invest time and love in you because they believe in your stability. Your next step is to learn to become exceedingly comfortable with their belief in you. This can become one of the missions in your life; it will bring great abundance, a wealth of quality friends and a loving relationship that has that perfect flavor of forever.

NOTES TO MY ANGELS:

ASPECT EIGHT

Humanology

ASPECT EIGHT
— Humanology —

77

We are at the place in human existence where a race between 'ignorance being blissful & enlightenment being essential' is in full swing. To use the whole human system is an absolute must at this point in our evolution. The common belief of yesterday and today is: we have a body and when the body stops life is over. Because of this belief system, life is considered a fragile event and all the sensations of life are extremely insecure. With the sensations of life being fragile, everything about it is considered critical and unsafe . . . this is the driving motivation of today's human world.

In this environment: job is critical; family is critical; religious belief is critical; culture is critical. Where is the motivation for joy when it is all viewed from such a critically fragile posture? There is very little enjoyment in the world today . . . there is a whole lot of fear. If you teach otherwise; you are considered foolish, naive and irresponsible.

To transcend from this fragile belief system — where everything is a battle and every discussion an argument — to a robust belief system where life is eternal and joy is essential . . . this is the required phenomenon. Inside the DNA of every animal there is a dominant nature developed for the purpose of survival. This survival trigger is set in place to insure that such "foolish" and "irresponsible" transitions — and the conversations that inspire them do not take place. But, there is also a driving force inside our human nature which suspects there is something much greater. This has set up the battle inside every human heart. This is the world today, in transition from survival driven by fear — to purpose driven by joy.

You cannot easily put this transition into words; you cannot easily describe your feelings about it, but you know it is right here . . . right now. Today, this sensation of something greater than what we are pursuing is very close to the surface.

The mystics and yogis called this sensation our 'Immortal Authority'. The mystery schools taught it to the chosen few. Now it is to be taught openly and publicly. It gives life an attitude of safety within any insecurity and a sense of greater purpose and fulfillment within any sense of slavery. To shift from the body orientation, with all its emphasis on being fragile – temporal – with massive insecurity and being surrounded by dangerous enemies, to a belief in our immortal authority would be huge. It is like a frog switching from being a polliwog to being the amphibian . . . from gills breathing water to lungs breathing air, a massive amount of courage is required.

We have so many unrealistic concepts attached to our beliefs, but if we shift this too rapidly our fears will rebel. We will feel lost without our safety nets. The entire emotional economy that is calibrated on the greed of our survival will collapse. There is a tremendous risk in bringing about world peace . . . a lot more than just the peace itself.

This transition . . . this new evolution is rooted in a hundred thousand years of development. We have conceptualized life with a collection of opinions based in emotions with very little reality. Our conceptualized GOD without the experiences of GOD is even at risk. This is at the root of our current wars.

Changing this is an adult conversation pleading to take place, but the world is quite childish . . . not prepared for such maturity. We may all want this adult conversation, but there are precious few adults to have it with. That is why you feel out of place; you might feel lonely from time to time. You have — in fact — been assigned to a toddler's center called planet Earth. Do not disrupt the toddlers with your negative judgments . . . simply make certain that you gather the like minded tribe.

To work effectively with the world as it is we have to be consistent, determined, compassionate, patient, intelligent and intuitive. We will require all this strength to guide the massive immaturity through this narrow opportunity in timespace. We are in a race between ignorance being blissful and enlightenment being essential. This is why it is said, "Let us gather in the company of people of love so we will remember our purpose in their presence."

The transition is right now . . . the time is right on . . . the race is here. Use your whole human system to join in this race . . . Angels are waiting to assist you in every way . . . using them for our highest purpose is of the essence.

NOTES TO MY ANGELS:

78

Three hundred years ago Guru Gobind Singh, a great master and the 10th Guru of the Sikhs, said, "If you want to walk on the path of love . . . place your head in your hands and walk with the courage of your heart."

This describes the most conscious stage of total commitment. This is the stage of the conscious adult and it is a stage of the heart,

Likewise, if you are on this path of compassionate consciousness, do not get caught up in the nets of doubt. These nets are not real; doubt comes up in developmental stages as avoidance. As a courageous, conscious, compassionate adult you are riding on an unbridled and unsaddled horse in the midst of an unproven purpose. With your doubt, you are asking for more proof . . . testing to see if your purpose is real or even possible. This proof as a means of overriding your doubt will not take place. True purpose must be an intentional step of pure faith. Just like love, and just like commitment — none of these — not your faith, not your love, and definitely not your commitment can use guarantees to prove their value. Nothing other than you — as you — can ever provide for these moments of mastery.

Never wait for anyone to test or prove your purpose to know that it is safe, secure and successful. You will end up dragging this net of doubt through the world as a symbol of great effort, but it is not. You talk about the fantasy of your purpose, but fear to walk about it. This is a person stuck at the stage of development that appears to be an adult, (age, body size, etc.) but is still a child. This adult-child stage is required; we all pass through it on the path from spiritual beginnings toward ultimate mastery. This is a stage to pass through, not live in.

Knowing that this path of mastery, self-realization and liberation is going to be a very wild ride — you might pause and avoid the ride with your doubt. You are the adult-child . . . you require more baking in the oven of time. This is not a bad pause or an unwanted stage. Use this time to practice on the details in order to perfect them. It can last for a very long time . . . consuming your entire life if you allow it to. Use this time as a tool, but do not setup camp here and make it your life. This stage between chronological childhood and spiritual adulthood is essential, and since the traditional 'rite of passage' is so universally missing from our modern culture, this adult-child stage is the replacement. Be good, be kind, and be compassionate with this stage . . . as you would with any child's fear or doubt. Do not analyze it, or misjudge it, but be determined to compassionately work through it. Be a forgiving mentor whenever you find this confusion within yourself or in others.

If you are in fact a conscious, compassionate, spiritual adult; then following the safe more proven standards will never satisfy your adult requirements for adventure. These are like trainer wheels on a bike — they will only slow you down if you already know how to ride. If however, you still find yourself searching for a guarantee of safety or success, and then you sense that this search feels unfitting of your evolutionary level . . . clear away this dabbling with heartfelt courage. Become the guarantee itself. Be your own faith and commitment. This is the stage of conscious adult consciousness.

Some will resist such a commitment in favor of their confusion and its tireless analysis. Know that these persons are committed to being an adult-child and there is nothing wrong with this stage of their development. You must however, draw the important conclusion that this behavior has no response ability (word spelled as such on purpose). Do not set up the dis — appointment of giving this adult-child the keys to the "car" of your life. They will not have the awareness or the commitment to manage such profound response ability - selflessly.

Learn to surround yourself with a balanced mix of conscious adults, adult-childs, and children. Each of these has a role to play in every one's world. Do not mislabel anyone with your false need for their approval. Live on purpose even when it is wild, untamed and unfinished . . . even when it is not approved of. Adults will understand this and appreciate the inspiration — adult-childs will question and judge and analyze and continue to go about their confusion. This is their way of testing and ultimately clearing their own path for growth. When you expect nothing more from them; they are free to be who they are destined to be, without the intimidating burden of your unhelpful criticism.

If you are truly on the path of love and commitment —not lust and confusion; place your heart above your head and walk with unbridled and unproven purpose. Gather many adults close around you and be a mentor to the adult-childs who are attracted to your fearless wisdom. Do not be enchanted by their attractions —or confused by their distractions. Remain committed to your purpose as a leader, as a teacher, as an adult in this, the next evolution.

NOTES TO MY ANGELS:

79

THE SETTING: A metaphor in the present time . . . You are the teacher in a classroom of twenty young children. There are nineteen dedicated students in the room and one dedicated screamer. Who captures the attention of the class . . . the teacher, the subjects, or the screamer?

When friends gather around you, and angels sing about you, and the seven blue ethers weave deep missions in the fabric of your psyche . . . . . then, a few people (of this Earth and in your World) speak out strongly against you . . . what is the final calculation? Who captures your attention? What is the score?

It sounds like a total victory for your good name . . . for sure it must be. But if those who would speak against you, are speaking very loudly; the outcome is always in question. You will have to be increasingly silent to hear and disciplined to bear witness to the gentler voices of the friends, the angels and the ethers praising your many victories.

Instincts beg you to holler — to return to your survival . . . compassion begs your quiescence — to return to your joy.

Friends, angels and ethers sing praises at a much higher frequency, with a subtler melody, and a softer volume. To hear this praise and truly relate to it in the midst of criticism; one must be devoted to the positive; disciplined to only hear the negative, but not be controlled by it; and dedicated to experiencing life's full spectrums — not just the loudest voices.

At such moments, with this proper outlook, all criticism takes its appropriate place . . . just a single seat within the registry of life in the classroom Earth. Then critics do not overwhelm the system. The negation and perhaps screaming, does not capture all of the attention. Breaths, meant to experience joy, are not condemned to only hear the one screaming child in the room. Your efforts to learn and grow can now be more balanced and rewarding, but always be aware that the screaming child sits inside you too.

What joy exists within a world of balance! What profoundness is able to gather with a sense of growth around this far more mature and conscious response ability! What clear pathways point toward your success . . . where challenges and obstacles once dominated! The nineteen devoted students within you are now set free to learn from each lesson of life, without being tormented by the hollers of the one fear or doubt. This metaphor is very real . . . meeting it daily (moment to moment) on real terms is essential.

NOTES TO MY ANGELS:

80

Today humanity finds itself sleep-walking through a concept of life . . . not living life itself. We have developed this conceptual life that isn't life in an evolutionary search for pleasure, and to protect ourselves from the every day pains of experience. Extremism attempts to pierce this numbness, but it is a failed reaction.

Ironically, this has become a very painful cul-de-sac (a dead-end of sorts): with food that is not food; medicine that is not medicine; beliefs that are not believable, controlled by feelings that are not our feelings and thoughts that are not our thoughts. They are composite drawings of some joys, hopes, fears, angers and doubts — mixed up with anticipations reacting to the joys, hopes, fears, angers and doubts of other's.

Life has become the media driving our anticipations by comparing someone else's memories to all our present day fantasies . . . a far cry from experiencing the experience of living life. We are actually having a virtual walk through of the showroom life that we are supposed to be experiencing.

We avoid experiencing where we are at, because we have developed a belief that it is not what we should be or want to be. Our life, always compared by the marketing power of media — where satisfaction does not sell products discontent sells product, stumbles sideways in search of some forward looking consumable. In this comparison driven dilemma we feel wrong . . . we hate being wrong, so we avoid 'being' altogether. We live in a concept of living, while we are in fact avoiding the very starting line of life. Externalized and disconnected from our life, we cannot even begin.

You, as your present identity, arrived with a consciousness – collected, nourished and grown — through thousands of progressive incarnations. Your destination — the true identity of your incarnation — is your journey from where you are (fate), to who you are (destiny). The ancients called it rasayana; a Sanskrit word for the path of pure essence . . . using innocence to locate your inner-sense and arrive at some common sense while experiencing life.

There are only two promises you must bring to this journey:
(1) I accept the starting point of where I am . . . and, (2) I believe I am authorized to reach my destiny. Set up a personal daily practice of yoga, conscious breathing

while walking, and meditation. Move one small step forward every day and measure your progress after each day, week month and particularly every forty days. Celebrate your experiences when you succeed and also when you fail.

Remember: failures are very important steps toward your goal . . . the goal of your destiny. Failures pave the roadways to every success. This is the lifestyle of our new evolution . . . it is very much alive for you today.

NOTES TO MY ANGELS:

81

Our life-destiny is conceived through the confluence of three (what yogis call) rivers — the Cosmological River (path of the soul's incarnations); the Genealogical River (path of the bloodline—the family tree); and the Experiential River (path of this lifetime's experiences).

Our DNA controls the Genealogical River and this river contributes one-third of our path to destiny. Bio-chemically: DNA consists of two polymer spirals (the double helix); the structure is made of sugar crystals (known as glycosylases) and salt crystals (known as phosphates). These crystals are joined together by enzymes using their electro-magnetic interactions.

What does this mean in terms of a human experience? At the most basic level it means DNA crystals carry on your life's observations, sensations and conversations using these crystals to transmit sub-chemical energies of electricity, magnetism, and light . . . In the deepest levels of this conversation, DNA is an optical (light-based) system . . . the microscopic salt and sugar crystals refract, reflect, magnify or de-magnify specific frequencies from the full light spectrum.

These frequencies carry the meaning, the purpose and the evolving nature of your bloodline through timespace. This is the nature of the physical body. It carries the consciousness throughout life. The human body is the highest and most evolved instrument for working with this procession of consciousness.

There is a subtle message being broadcast here; your DNA, along with this message present identity to your consciousness. It is a light based system of color and a sound based system of tones (Shabd in Sanskrit). Through the pressures this sound creates, it generates electro-magnetic fields which control and move the angles of the microscopic salt and sugar crystals. These crystals then work with the angles of light to move the messages. The clarity is increased or decreased; the understanding is increased or decreased; the comprehension is increased or decreased and the whole system experiences the experience or does not. You are either growing or you are not.

Our consciousness determines where we are (our progress) within this massive procession of evolution. Remember: consciousness is the only part of you that travels with you from life-time to life-time. It is a marker of your evolutionary soul progress. The ultimate goal of all this progression is to become the messenger of the message that all things have a profound unity — all things are one. This is GOD consciousness.

Since sound controls these crystals, they are directly affected by the sounds of your words, all your emotions and feelings, all your thoughts, perceptions and opinions and all your attitudes. Discipline, discipline, discipline . . . this is the reason we practice yoga, chant mantras, recite prayers (grace before meals), sing songs of inspiration, sing songs of love, recite banis (sacred prayers of the enlightened ones), read scriptures (sacred writings of the enlightened ones). We do all of this to discipline our sounds. This is why there are so many diverse practices and ways of disciplining the sounds we make with our voices and with our thoughts. This is why it is so important to speak properly, apologize rapidly, forgive quickly and evolve your being and inspire others.

Take the time to discipline yourself and grow in excellence and consciousness so that your life is fulfilled and becomes an inspiration to all who meet you. This is your greatest possible fulfillment of life.

NOTES TO MY ANGELS:

82

As a child . . . the tools of childhood served us well. These . . . the tools of doubt; jealousy; envy; frustration; fear; fascination; unreasonable humor and many, many others all provided the illusion of security and stimulated our childhood growth. As an adult we must put aside many of these tools except unreasonable humor (belly laughing) and fascination: otherwise, the other ones will hold us way back, disrupt our sacred perceptions of life, create disharmony amongst our peers and produce other unintended consequences.

For example; doubt as a child's tool serves the child to further examine and then gain understanding of the road ahead — a road that the child measures inch by inch for the purposes of negotiating with fear and affording the illusion of security. Arrogance — a tool of childhood — steps in to overcome this doubt — becomes the mover and driver through the formative years.

As an adult — not just a chronological one, but an authentic one — we are to travel through the years — not inch by inch, but dream by dream . . . accomplishment by accomplishment. Any doubt slows this progress way down and becomes a blockage to the joys of progress. As a spiritually evolved adult — a path-walker as it is known to the ancients — the journey of an enlightened adult's life is to be measured in light years. Doubt and all the other childhood tools are disastrous and virtually unusable at this rate of journey. The preferred tools of this advanced evolution are tools of elegance and grace, integrity and courage; there is no place for arrogance; there is no place for power struggles; there is no place for the deceptions caused by fear, jealousy, envy and insecurity.

By this measure, the world today appears to be primarily populated with aging, adult sized children. This is the current nature of life on our planet and it is not only the problem . . . it is in fact by design. As a teacher, you must learn to work with this design, master it and become a mentor to all these adult-children (known as adult-childs). This is the role for your advanced consciousness; this is the road of your advanced mastery. You are not to become frustrated, or hurt, or disappointed, or wrestle for control; those are the tools of childhood and they will not serve you here. They will only create struggle when dealing with the adult-childs. Instead — seeing the world as it is — become responsible . . . able to respond to the way it is.

Right here, right now; have an adult response. See the way things are in this world and in your world. If that means making a move to set the playing field back to level for all the adult-childs around you — then do not hesitate. Make the move! Create the time of your life and their lives! Remain committed to your purpose as a leader, as a teacher, as an adult in this one-room schoolhouse Earth . . . the new evolutionary human consciousness . . .

NOTES TO MY ANGELS:

83

The quantum laws of physics live vivaciously within the nature of humanology, but science, even today, has discovered only minute amounts of this magic that yogis have known of and lived by for centuries. Science has yet to allow this magical half of the cosmos to raise its own voice amongst the deafening roar of the logic . . . "law-gic".

Learn to work with the magical half of this multi-verse as well as the prevailing logical half. Be a source-knower — become a source-seer . . . know and see what will cause the world of your world to evolve more rapidly than ever. Release every limitation, every small biased thought; release every presentation that prevents the extraordinary.

Because the world that is happening to you is happening through you . . . the observed and the observer become the same event and manifest the power of thought. When you observe this without judgment, you leave this neutral attitude within the collective human potential and humanity becomes more prosperous. When you observe the world at large without judgment, you leave a blessing.

Any judgment traps the world in the exact way being judged . . . forgiveness moves and releases the traps forward to a new moment. Forgiveness is the antidote to judgment, far closer to the way you wish. Use this magical power of observation to become a healer of your world. You will notice that discomfort — even disease — is like a hand full of sand . . . when you observe it closely you will notice that all of the parts are always in motion. This motion is able to transmute the discomfort into comfort; the sickness into healing . . . every action creates equal reaction.

Even in the case of serious disease, the ease is equally available right next to it. Acknowledge this ease; acknowledge the comfort — the comfort and ease will acknowledge you back . . . will become more active. Remember: energy flows where your attention goes. Focus your attention on that which will heal . . . feed the ease — nourish the comfort . . . the blessings of this world are right there at your thought-tips, the new evolution of human consciousness . . .

NOTES TO MY ANGELS:

84

The world is the reflection of your journey; you hear this time and again on the spiritual path. What this means is that when you are in a room of people, a boardroom of associates, a train of strangers, a moment of circumstances — all are reflecting an angle of a facet of you. Could be the present you, the future you or the past you; whatever is projected is reflected at the speed of light. In life, just as in the hall of mirrors; many of the reflections may distort or magnify all or parts of the projection, but within each reflection (distorted or not) there is reality, there is clarity. The total reflection may not seem true, but it contains truth. Even when the reflection is a distortion, it is up to you to find the seeds of truth within the sea of distortion.

To believe in such a dynamic law and lead your life within this phenomenon is of course a great risk; it can deeply disturb a slumbering consciousness. Remember, when nothing is ventured nothing is ever gained. Even walking is a great risk . . . it is in fact simply falling and then catching yourself from falling with each step. As a very young child you were first confronted be the risk of walking; as you decided to try it, you were filled with fear. Then you were somehow inspired to see it as a risk worth taking . . . there were sufficient rewards to be gained at the end of the walk. Now, as you walk about your days, you don't even perceive the slightest degree of the actual risk.

You won't . . . until you become very, very old and once again connect to the same risk of walking you knew as a child. The reality is that the risk was always there, it never left; you were always falling and then catching yourself from falling with each step. Your attitude simply changed; the inspiration overpowered the trepidation. Now the trepidation again catches up with the inspiration and questions it.

Losing the sense of risk is the ultimate step in any natural progression . . . when acquiring any skill, achieving any goal. The same is true in seeing the world as your own reflection, for seeing the world as your reflection is ultimately the most powerful skill you can gain. It is time to develop this same "risk-free" relationship with such a risk. This is the risk that surrounds every one of your life-goals, every one of your fondest dreams. This is the skill known as star-walking and it is only accomplished by those who are willing to pursue the inspiration in the face of tremendous trepidation. You will be given many opportunities to practice . . . take the chances you are gifted.

o   First: see all the risks in viewing the entire world as your reflection; do not deny any of them.

o   Second: see the goal as absolutely worthwhile.

o   Third: see that this risk of viewing the world as your reflection creates every fear that stands between you and your dreams.

o   Fourth: refocus on the inspiration of the goal and slightly angle the view that sits beside the risk . . . just see it as part of the landscape . . . then a little less . . . and a little less.

These risks — just as the risks in walking — will never go away. Your relationship with them changes. Your attitude simply shifts on which is more important — the inspirations or the trepidations.

NOTES TO MY ANGELS:

ASPECT NINE

Spiritual
Community

ASPECT NINE
—Spiritual Community—

85

When you sincerely request to grow spiritually — life will take and lead you through the unknown, unfamiliar and uncertain barrios of this world. In this, you will be tested, taunted and tormented in order to surrender and become completely 'OK' with the total lack of security and feeling safe. How else are you going to become introduced to elegance of your faith?

Safe, after all, is different for each person — it is defined by the individual's karmic cycle of consciousness. With some, safe is being able to make up their own decisions; for others, safe is to have all decisions made for them. All persons have their standard, but unless something knocks you off your safe-zone, you will hold on to it for dear life and never grow. This safe-zone is then the most dangerous place to live. It will keep you attached to the illusions generated by your karmic cycle (the sum total of your incarnate scores). If you want to change and grow from where you already are: you must dramatically shift what you have already done.

But even this is not enough to grow spiritually. There are so many places for your fears and doubts to hide and hold you to the known qualities of your safety. This is known as shakti-path and is where a spiritual teacher is essential . . . a person to knock you off this pedestal of your false certainty. Your ego and your sense of danger will fight tooth and nail. One thing to remember: even if you are not enjoying the ride — in order to grow, you must ride the ride.

Karmic cycles are conditions of your cosmology (cycle of your Soul) and it is perfectly supported by your genealogy (cycle of your ancestors the family's physical and emotional DNA). Reinvesting your family's emotions into your own body at a cellular level; you renew this karmic stumbling block from your bloodline. This need to be cleared and overcome — either by you, or later on by your children, your grand-children, your great-grand-children, or further down the evolutionary line.

'Safe' is a state of consciousness, not a comforting thought, not a creatable condition, not the fulfillment of an emotional need or even a negotiation; it is not even an action orientation. Requiring the feeling of safety is a most dangerous state of unconsciousness. Unless a moratorium is declared on worry, there will always be a "good" and convincing reason for worrying about "what ifs" and, "what might becomes".

Commitment and surrender are the only roads through such insecurity . . . this for the simple reason, commitment has the power to trump all other emotions and feelings. Commitment is a form of moratorium . . . a dedication to override all the reasons for anything but success. Commitment gives you a certain caliber . . . and this caliber gives you a certain character . . . and this character gives you a certain capacity to uphold any and all declarations. Back to point: the mere fact that you have declared a desire to grow, brings this in your face to be resolved once and for ever. Then, when you are walking through Hell on your way to Heaven, do not stop walking. As you step into the 'Unknown' — walking through the unknown confusion and uncertainty — trust that you are still a part of the known Universe. After all, there is no way out or around our Universe. Walk on the middle path, the one right in the middle of your extremes — on the one side you are deathly afraid to move and on the other side you are trying to run away from perceived danger and on to safety. Both of these are cycles of illusion and ignorance, but in the clutches of them there is no convincing.

Meditate with great discipline into the source-code at the core of your bones to correct with this reality at the root. Make a daily routine and if you have the opportunity, relate to a teacher who will not let you slide. Take up this courage with surrender and commitment and face your insecurities until you no longer feel unsafe. You have begun the journey . . . this is spiritual growth. You will know when you have reached progress because it is then that you will not feel safe and it will not feel unsafe . . . it just feels like it feels.

This is a huge contribution to yourself, to your bloodline and to humanity. Moving beyond your need for safety and into the arms of surrender and commitment, trumps all the elements that have held every one back for lifetimes. You are now the hominid — the two-legger — graduating toward being humanely human. Give yourself a big hand and a huge hug. Bank on this — this is the new economy in the new evolution. This is true prosperity (pro-spirit). This is spiritual growth.

NOTES TO MY ANGELS:

86

We do not inherit the world from our ancestors; we borrow it from our children. Evolution expands with every generation in order for the universe to survive and thrive. Children are the only future of this planet's human life. To produce a future where children are courageously inspired to confidently generate positive lives . . . lives committed to peaceful solutions and sustainable environments — this will require all of our conscious efforts.

In order to secure this future we must learn from the past. Remember the old saying that history is written and rewritten to manage the victory of the victors. Well, this is the management of ignorance . . . plain and simple . . . and we cannot afford this anymore. In today's world there are so many ways in which this ignorance is propagated and our human brain-power is abandoned in the process. The only time humanity feels disconnected, combative and competitive for resources is when ignorance eliminates our sense of cooperation and global community. We must leave these ancient – stone-age — competitive constructs behind, and develop — for our children and the generations to follow — a compassionate, compatible future.

If you are reading this you came by it because you are one of the pioneers of the future of this exact world. We are here to abandon ignorance; we are here to make information universally available; we are here to increase awareness and produce a global human community in the process. We are here to reduce the entertainment of consumption and increase the attainment of enlightenment. We are here to utilize the vast human neurology for the purpose of discovery and send our children into a future of hope, enthusiasm and peace. We are here to make a difference, not just make a living. We are here to pay back the debt we have created for the future . . . for our children. We are not here to make believe . . . we are here to believe we can make it.

We are the pioneers of the future . . . we are a global human community . . . we entrain ourselves with enlightenment.

NOTES TO MY ANGELS: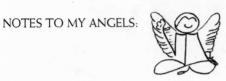

87

Through this journey of life there are many levels of consciousness. At the most microscopic levels of observation, liquid crystals make up the angles of consciousness. This is why physical flexibility is so important when working on consciousness . . . liquids are the most flexible of all substances and the crystals of your DNA respond to this flexibility with great enthusiasm. In fact, these crystals are perfectly arranged and held in their liquid positions by the exact level of human consciousness . . . to be either maintained in place, degenerated to reassess, or regenerated and progressed to advance the life. Every thought, word and deed of your lifetime contributes to this process.

We have now evolved to a cosmic season of human fulfillment and practical enlightenment . . . the time of high nature. This is the time when the harmonies of our world are at their peak. It is the time to join these harmonic forces that surround us and do so with complete confidence. Learn to tune into their power, their accuracy and their momentum.

Simply look around yourself and you can see there is the natural harmony of the elements (earth, water, fire, air and ether) always moving into alignment with each other. There is the harmony of the plants growing into adulthood around each other. There is the harmony of the animals raising their young to fulfill every evolutionary destiny. There is the harmony of the space that has been set aside for us humans to cooperate and collaborate in. This last one — the advantageous space of human cooperation — this is the one that has been ignored by the competitive industrial movement. Indigenous people know all about this advantage; they follow it with their nutrition, with their medicine, with their relationships to the Earth and to each other. They use it to fulfill their lives.

This is the advantage that we ignored, undervalued and set aside — when the industrial revolution declared four hundred years ago, "We shall conquer nature." This is the same ignorance that is causing us so much trouble with pollution, corruption and disharmony at present. This is the ignorance that collapses trust in financial markets, produces diseases from our industrial inventions and uses war to search for peace.

Now is the time for people to move in tune with each other and take advantage of the advantage provided by nature, plants and animals. It is the season for people to synchronize with the world and mesh into the Divine construct. This is the time to be blessed, to feel blessed and to bless all endeavors, join forces with the creative common abundance surrounding everything and cooperate with its ventures and adventures.

In doing so, we will actually align with the nature of nature. This is the nature that prepares to fulfill every longing. This is the nature that confidently begins every preparation. This is the nature that finishes what is begun and succeed at each finish. This is the nature of nature in the season of fulfillment. Join with it and become the most extraordinary you . . .

NOTES TO MY ANGELS:

88

When you are dedicated to raising the food for your entire village . . . you will always eat. Accused of being over idealistic, you run the risk of being an answer to all humanities challenges. This is a wonderful dilemma to be caught up in. This can be a real purpose-filled driver in your life.

Remember however; when you take on these types of idealistic tasks there will always be push back both from without and within. The outside push back is obvious, but the internal ones are most clever. They create the foundation for your doubts, for your concerns . . . all the way up to your largest fears. They are rich earth for the internal ridicule and self defeating monologues that lurk in the shadows of the unconscious. They are always there waiting, just like mildew waits for dampness. You are not being targeted; don't take this personally . . . you are just an opportunity for either achievement or defeat. This is the nature of nature.

It is up to you to keep up; to keep yourself in the most conscious frame of mind. This is the duty of your daily practice . . . your Sadhana. How do you establish this practice? On whose back do you ride out into your world each day . . . your hero's back or the back of your naysayer . . . your inspiration's back or the back of your doubt? Make a conscious choice of the choice you make . . . every morning . . . every day.

Gestation and birthing of the spirit-body is much like that of the physical body. In fact, you are born into the physical body on Earth to continue the path of ultimately being born from the womb of this physical body into the spirit-body. When you have completed your path through the dense physical stages of life, you will cease incarnating on the physical planets of this multiverse we call a universe and move on to higher stages in less dense realms.

The stages of gestation and development of the spirit body — while in this physical "body-womb" — are much like their physical counterparts. When the ancient descriptions of these five stages translates into practical modern English, they sound like this: (1) Spirit-Embryo (the very earliest beginnings of the journey lasting thousands of lifetimes — no self-awareness); (2) Spirit-Fetal (the embryo has blossomed into self awareness, but is not yet born into the awareness of the oneness of all souls); (3) Spirit-Thresh-holder (birthing at the opening to the spirit-world of higher consciousness and aware of the oneness of all souls. This is a very early stage of spiritual life and there is much confusion, trepidation and duality); (4) Spirit-Path-walker (developing the deeper understanding and compassion of the path of the soul and committed to walking on this path); (5) Spirit-Star-walker (the enlightened — awakened masters leading life through the cosmos as they pass from the physical plane).

Everyone on Earth is on this path at some level. This world — as such — is a one room schoolhouse . . . every level being schooled and evolved together, each person learning at their appropriate level and rate. For this reason — as a leader — the most important quality to have in such an environment is complete non-judgment and total non-bias.

The ultimate goal of evolution is — to be alive in the physical body while being fully born into the spirit-body simultaneously. As the great Sikh sage and master — Guru Nanak — said, "Be dead while yet alive." In this state you are not dead physically, but you are also not controlled by the needs and wants of the physical world . . . in fact you are more fully alive than life has ever been imagined. You are highly disciplined and a shining example for others to follow.

This —birthing into spirit —was accomplished by all the Prophets, the Avatars, the Messiahs and the Masters throughout history. We have created many stories about these great ones and in these stories we have declared all they accomplished beyond our mortal capacity . . . which it is not. Their lives were an example of what we are all capable of achieving. It is the evolution of human consciousness and the goal of all life. **Now** is the time to take from their examples and continue this journey forward toward our common destiny.

We are all One.

NOTES TO MY ANGELS:

Postscript

This book wholeheartedly wishes you, your family and all whom you love and hold special and even those you don't know, the healthiest, happiest, holiest state of angelic grace today and in the years to come.
We wish this to the leaders of this Earth. We wish this to the suffering on this Earth. We wish this to the animals, the plants, and the minerals of this Earth. We wish this to the elementals, the Angels and the future of this Earth.

REMEMBER: The *HOW* always appears within a sufficient *WHY*. . .
Angels are great at coming up with the sufficient reason WHY . . .
it is like second nature to them. Utilize this leverage of trust to make every other sensation and emotion more effective.

Take the inspiration of these Angels and enable yourself to be healthy, happy, holy, strong, vital, safe and conscious to achieve your goals that evolve your mission and fulfill your destiny with every breath, sip, bite, step, drive and flight you take in the company of loving people to remember your purpose in their presence. Angels have a favorite saying to help us remember this which you must read aloud: I am ready willing and able now . . . to be all that I was born to be . . . to fulfill my eternal destiny . . . liberate my entire family into our immortal authority.

Set your expectations as high as you can imagine, then work daily to activate them. Do not let life become the accumulations of, "I'll do it tomorrow." Become aware of the Earth's collective pain momentarily and daily . . . do not dwell in it monumentally, but make a place in your heart for relieving it. When you can't be the solution at least become the compassion.

Upon awakening every morning . . . bow down in the deepest and humblest gratitude to the Infinite Divinity within you . . . now you are amongst the Angels while living on the Earth.

About The Author

Guru Singh DD, mss, is a third generation yogi and master-teacher of Humanology and Kundalini yoga and meditation. He is also a musician, composer, author, and Minister of Sikh Dharma with a Doctorate of Divinity. Most importantly to him however, he is a family man . . . with a base in Los Angeles, Seattle, and India, Guru Singh teaches throughout the world with his wife Guruperkarma Kaur. Together they have two children . . . a son Sopurkh and a daughter Hari Purkh.

Members of Guru Singh's family lived in India in the early 20th Century. This is where his Great-Aunt met Paramahansa Yogananda, author of Autobiography of a Yogi, in Calcutta in 1916. She studied and traveled with this spiritual master from India to America and served him until his passing in 1952. Guru Singh was born in Seattle in 1945 into this yogic household setting the foundation for a spiritual life from the age of zero.

In January of 1969, Guru Singh (then 23) met and began a thirty four year long daily study with the Master of Kundalini Yoga - Yogi Bhajan. Guru Singh, the first Westerner to wear the turban, began accompanying Yogi Bhajan as he taught at Universities, lecture halls, spiritual centers and Sikh Gurudwaras around the world.

As a minister, Guru Singh works with spiritual and religious leaders of nearly every faith, including the Dalai Lama on Seeds of Compassion and Sri Amma Bhagavan of Oneness University. He draws on his extensive musical background and knowledge of Sahaj Shabd (sound) therapy to offer a unique approach to counseling the natural human harmonies through meditation and applied sound. He is also involved with Dr. Dharma Khalsa and Dr. Andrew Newberg of the University of Pennsylvania, School of Medicine - Department of Neuro-Theology using medical imaging to measure dynamic brain function under the influence of meditation, mantra and prayer.

Guru Singh is one of the Founding Directors of the Miri Piri Academy—an international boarding school (K –12) in Amritsar, India. Here, students from around the world become global citizens and future leaders through an academic curriculum delivered with a spiritual focus. Serving on the boards of several fast growth companies, he is dedicated to transforming today's world of education, technology, media and community building. All connecting the over-arching vision and spiritual mission . . . reaching humanity personally, while teaching globally.

THE GURU SINGH
GLOBAL COMMUNITY

Join Guru Singh at http://blog.gurusingh.com/ for the daily
Inspirational Blessings; and at http://podcast.gurusingh.com/ for
Podcasts of current lectures.

Find a collection of his mantra CDs at http://music.gurusingh.com/
and participate in building a strong global community at
http://global.gurusingh.com/ . . .

Additional products by Guru Singh:

- **108 Ways to Great Days** – A journey through journaling – BOOK
As the ancient world grew through its evolutionary progression;
yogis, mystics and religious scholars discovered many celestial
measurements that involved the number 108. 108 evolved into a sacred
recurring theme in diverse spiritual and religious practices around the
world as the number of steps from ordinary human consciousness to
enlightenment. This book was designed by Guru Singh to have 108
distinct steps. Work with it and enjoy — first the process — then the
enlightening results.

- **The Guru Singh Experience Vol 1** // CD Available at www.cdbaby.com
  TRACKS: Ong So Hung, Har Haree, Ek Ong Kar
- **The Guru Singh Experience Vol 2** // CD Available at www.cdbaby.com
  TRACKS:: Ong Namo Guru Dev Namo, Humee Hum Brahm Hum,
  Aad Guray Nameh
- **Naad Mantra Vol 1** // CD Available at www.cdbaby.com
  TRACKS: Aap Sahai Hooaa, Guru Ram Das, Har Har Har Har Gobinday,
  Aad Such Jugaad Such, Pran Sutra
- **The Guru Singh Collection** (Guru Singh, Seal & Friends)
  // CD Available at www.cdbaby.com
  TRACKS: I Am,Humee Hum, Fortunate,Wahe guru Golden Temple Song
- **Game of Chants** (Guru Singh, Seal & Friends)
  // CD Available at www.spiritvoyage.com
- **Chantz 2 iMPAct Earth** (mantras to bring light to a troubled time)
  // CD Available at www.spiritvoyage.com

6604847R0

Made in the USA
Charleston, SC
12 November 2010